How to be an Outstanding Childminder

Also available from Continuum

Childminder's Guide to Child Development, Allison Lee

Childminder's Guide to Health & Safety and Child Protection, Allison Lee

Childminder's Guide to Play and Activities, Allison Lee

Childminder's Handbook, Allison Lee

Inside Guide to Being a Childminder, Allison Lee

How to be an Outstanding Childminder

Allison Lee

continuum

Continuum International Publishing Group
The Tower Building   80 Maiden Lane, Suite 704
11 York Road   New York
London   NY 10038
SE1 7NX

www.continuumbooks.com

British Library Cataloguing-in-Publication Data
A catalogue record for this book is available from the British Library.

ISBN: 9781847064967 (paperback)

Library of Congress Cataloging-in-Publication Data
Lee, Allison.
  How to be an outstanding childminder / Allison Lee.
      p. cm.
  ISBN 978-1-84706-496-7 (pbk.)
  1. Day care aides. 2. Day care aides–Certification–Great Britain. I. Title.

  HQ778.5.L439 2009
  362.71'2068–dc22

                                    2008037114

Typeset by YHT Ltd, London
Printed and bound in Great Britain by
Athenaeum Press Ltd., Gateshead, Tyne & Wear

Contents

Acknowledgements

I have been privileged to work with many different families over the past 14 years that I have been a childminder, and I would like to thank all of these families for allowing me to be a part of their family.

Introduction

Childminders have been caring for children successfully for many years, however parents are now, quite rightly, demanding a much higher quality childcare service for their children, and in many cases the Ofsted grading awarded to individual childminders is the only way of initially showing the adequacy of the childcare provision. Indeed many parents would not even consider a childminder who has not at least achieved a 'good' grading, and most are prepared to pay more money and travel further to secure a place with an 'outstanding provider'.

More than three years have passed since the introduction of the new grading system by Ofsted and still it is seen by many as being an exceptionally difficult feat to achieve the highest grading. This book, written by a practising childminder who has herself achieved an outstanding grade for her childcare service, shows how it is possible, with a little common sense and practical planning, to prove to the Ofsted inspector that you too are worthy of the highest grading.

Chapter One
Ofsted

The aims of the registration system

There is a legal requirement under the Children Act 2004 which states that anyone who looks after one or more children under the age of 8 years for more than two hours per day, for reward, must be registered with the Early Years Directorate of Ofsted in England or the Care Standards Inspectorate Registration in Wales. In Scotland the responsible body is the National Care Standards Committee, while in Northern Ireland it is local Health and Social Care Trusts. 'Reward' can be in the form of money or payment in kind, and 'domestic premises' are those which are used wholly or mainly as a private dwelling.

It will be necessary, when applying for registration, for you to be able to prove to your local department that your home meets the legal requirements to provide a safe and secure environment for the children you intend to care for.

You will need to demonstrate that you are a suitable person to provide care for young children and that you take your responsibilities seriously.

The registration system is in place so that the appropriate authority can aim to:

- Ensure that all childminders meet the standards of the Early Years Foundation Stage (EYFS)

- Protect children and provide reassurance for parents/ guardians

- Promote environments where children are safe and well cared for

- Ensure care contributes to development and learning

- Promote high-quality childcare provision.

The Early Years Foundation Stage is a central part of the government's ten-year childcare strategy *Choice for Parents, the Best Start for Children*. In recent years there have been a significant number of developments in the early years curriculum and standards. The EYFS builds on these developments and childminders need to recognize continuity with the principles, approach and pedagogy of the three frameworks previously worked towards: *The National Standards for Under 8s Daycare and Childminding, Birth to Three Matters* and the *Curriculum Guidance for the Foundation Stage*, all of which have been replaced by the EYFS and, from September 2008, have been repealed.

It is now mandatory for all schools and early years providers, including childminders, in Ofsted-registered settings attended by children from birth to the end of the academic year in which the child has their fifth birthday, to follow the EYFS framework.

The main aim of the EYFS is to help young children to achieve the five *Every Child Matters* outcomes, which are:

- Staying safe
- Being healthy
- Enjoying and achieving
- Making a positive contribution
- Achieving economic well-being.

Exercise: Taking into account the five *Every Child Matters* outcomes, think about ways in which you can successfully achieve each of these. Make a list of how you can encourage children to stay safe, be healthy, enjoy and achieve, make a positive contribution and achieve economic well-being while they are in your setting.

The EYFS aims to achieve these outcomes by:

- Setting the standards
- Providing for equality of opportunity
- Creating the framework for partnership working
- Improving quality and consistency
- Laying a secure foundation for future learning.

Let us now look more closely at the ways Ofsted propose to help young children achieve the five *Every Child Matters* outcomes.

Setting the standards – It is essential that childminders understand that they have an important role to play in the early years experiences of the children in their care. The EYFS sets standards which enable childminders and other early years providers to reflect the varied, personalized and abundant experiences offered in the home setting. It is important that practitioners, like parents, deliver individualized learning, development and care which provide children with the best possible start in life. Young children need the necessary individual support in order for them to make progress at their own speed and achieve their full potential.

Providing for equality of opportunity – Childminders have a responsibility to ensure positive attitudes towards diversity and difference within their setting in order to ensure that every child feels welcome and is included, and in order for them to learn to value diversity in others from the earliest possible age. It is vital that all children in the early years setting, irrespective of ethnicity, culture, religion, family background, disabilities, learning difficulties, gender, ability or language should have equal opportunity to experience a wealth of challenging and enjoyable methods of learning and development.

Childminders need to focus on:

- Removing barriers which may already exist.
- Being knowledgeable about the early signs of needs which may lead to later difficulties, and being confident in responding to these signs quickly and effectively – involving appropriate agencies where necessary.
- Challenging children and extending their abilities.

Creating the framework for partnership working – In order for the EYFS to be delivered successfully it is essential that childminders understand the importance of working in partnership with parents and other professionals. If children receive education and care in more than one setting, for example pre-school or nursery, in addition to the childminding setting, practitioners must ensure continuity and coherence whereby relevant information is shared amongst each setting and with the parents. Childminders need to remember that parents are central to their child's well-being, and as such, working closely with the parents of the children you are caring for should be a priority in order to identify children's learning needs and to ensure a quick response to any particular area of difficulty.

Improving quality and consistency – By ending the distinction between care and learning for children aged from birth to 3 years and 3 to 5 years, the EYFS has brought together and simplified the learning and development and welfare requirements of all children from birth to 5 years. As most requirements of the EYFS are applicable to all types of early years settings, parents can be reassured that their children will receive continuity of care and essential standards of provision regardless of which type of setting they choose for their child.

Laying a secure foundation for future learning – The early years of a child's life are crucial to their future success, and it is important that their earliest experiences encourage them to build a firm foundation on which to base their future learning. Although it is important that children are stretched in order to reach their full potential, childminders need to be aware of the age and stage of development each child in their care is currently at in order to plan and provide suitable activities and learning experiences, without pushing the child beyond their own personal capabilities. In order to be able to achieve this factor successfully childminders need to undertake continual observational assessments of the children in their care in order to plan for each child's continuing development through enjoyable, play-based activities. They need to take a flexible approach which enables them to respond rapidly to the child's continually changing learning and development needs and ensure that the child's experiences away from the setting, for example, at home, are related to, and incorporated in, what the child is learning in the childminding setting.

The grading system

In April 2005 Ofsted announced that they would change some of the ways in which they inspect childcare settings in England. One of the areas of change is the grading system. Prior to 2005, childminders' inspection reports stated that the childcare service provided was either 'good', 'satisfactory' or 'unsatisfactory'. The grading proved unpopular and confusing and it was replaced with a new, four-tier scale of:

Grade 1: Outstanding – Given to exceptional settings that have excellent outcomes for children.

Grade 2: Good – Given to strong settings that are effective in promoting outcomes for children.

Grade 3: Satisfactory – Given to settings that have acceptable outcomes for children but which have scope for improvement.

Grade 4: Inadequate – Given to weak settings that have unacceptable outcomes for children.

In addition to the changes in the grading scale, Ofsted also decided to give shorter notice periods prior to inspections and to introduce a simple self-evaluation element to the inspection (see Chapter 3).

Inspection frameworks for childcare are now more in line with those of schools and colleges, and reports will focus on what it is like to be a child in each particular day-care setting. In order for the inspector to judge the overall quality of the care each childminder provides, Ofsted inspectors will base their decisions on how well you meet a series of outcomes for children which are set out in the Green Paper *Every Child Matters*, and are now in the Children Act 2004.

Inspectors also base their assessments on how well you organize your childcare to help promote children's well-being and look at whether you meet the appropriate standards for learning, development and care.

Few people, no matter how good the service they provide, or how many years' experience they may have in childcare, relish the idea of an inspection. The idea of having your work assessed, your moves monitored and your words scrutinized can fill even the most confident childminder with dread. However, inspections are a vital part of your work as a childminder and it is essential that you plan properly for your Ofsted inspection to ensure the best possible outcome for yourself and your business – one of an outstanding nature!

It is probably fair to say that your home and work will already be scrutinized on a daily basis, probably without you even realizing it, when parents drop off and collect their children. No matter how tired and harassed the parent may be don't be fooled into thinking they will not notice if *you* are short tempered, or if your house is dirty or the children are unhappy. They will, and most importantly, they should! If your business lives up to the watchful eye of your parents then you should rest assured that Ofsted will have an equally high opinion of your provision. However, it is vital that you are aware of the nature of the inspection and do your utmost to ensure that you are prepared for this vital part of your job as a childcare practitioner.

Regulations and legislation

Ofsted regulates childminders using the following four methods:

- Registration
- Inspection
- Investigation
- Enforcement.

Registration – This process covers checks on you and your premises together with any other adults who live or work on the premises where you intend to carry out your childminding service.

Inspection – Ofsted inspectors will carry out checks on your childminding service periodically. You will be issued with a report setting out their findings and any actions they feel you must take. This report must be made available to parents.

Investigation – An Ofsted inspector may carry out an investigation into your childcare provision to check that you are meeting all the necessary standards and requirements within the EYFS.

Enforcement – If necessary, Ofsted can take action against you if you are not meeting the statutory framework for the EYFS.

Disqualifications

Every person wishing to become a registered childminder must meet the standards and conditions set out by Ofsted. However, there are certain factors that may disqualify you from becoming registered and if this is the case you will not be able to become a childminder.

Your registration may be disqualified if you or any person who lives or works with you has been:

1   Put on the Protection of Children Act List which considers a person unsuitable to work with children

2   Convicted or charged with any offence against a child

3   Convicted or charged with certain offences against an adult

4   Listed on the Department for Children, Schools and Family Education and Employment List 99 which considers a person not fit and proper to work with children.

Chapter Two
Professionalism

Understanding the requirements of registration

There are certain requirements you will have to prove that you can meet prior to Ofsted agreeing to grant registration. Ofsted will be looking for the ways in which you can demonstrate the following:

- How you comply with the necessary standards for learning, development and care for children from birth to 5 years of age.

- That you agree to comply with any regulations and conditions which your regulatory body may feel necessary to impose on you.

- That you are a suitable person to look after children under the age of 8 years and that any other person working with you is also suitable.

- That every person living or employed on the premises are suitable to be in regular contact with children under the age of 8 years.

- That the premises where you intend to carry out your childminding business are suitable for the purpose of caring for children under the age of 8 years.

It is essential that, in addition to complying with the standards, regulations and conditions imposed on your registration, you also ensure that you notify Ofsted of any:

- Alterations to your premises or childcare provision
- Changes to any assistants, employees or family circumstances
- Circumstances which may affect the welfare of any children in your care.

NB There are some factors that would automatically prevent you from becoming a registered childminder (see Chapter 1).

The flow chart on the next page shows the basic steps of the application process which you will have to go through in order for a decision to be made as to whether you may become a registered childminder.

We will now look at the steps outlined in the flow chart in more detail so that you will be aware of what is involved during your application process and what will be required from you.

Information and application pack issued/returned and checks

To obtain an information pack you should contact your local authority. They will also furnish you with details of pre-registration briefing sessions and information about registration courses and training. You should also request copies of the Practice Guidance for the Early Years Foundation Stage and the Statutory Framework for the Early Years Foundation Stage when applying for your application pack, and read these carefully before applying to become registered.

The application pack contains general information regarding the

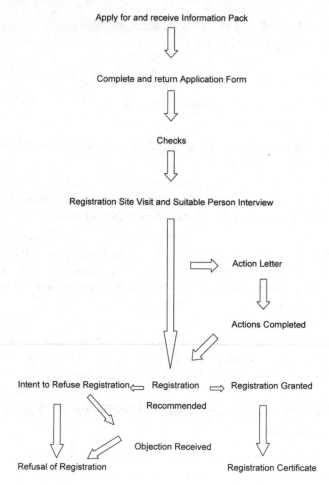

Fig 2.1 *The registration process*

childminding registration process together with the following four forms:

1 CM1 – This form requests information about you and the premises where you intend to operate your childminding business from.

2   CM2 – This form asks for a declaration about criminal records and matters of suitability to care for young children, and also asks for your consent for Ofsted to make checks with certain other professionals including:

Social Services (child protection register, social service records)
Your General Practitioner
Police Officers/Criminal Records Bureau
Protection of Children's Act List
Department for Education and Skills List 99
Referees
Previous employers
Health Visitor
The Registered Homes List.

3   Health Declaration Form.

4   Police Check Form – As you are requesting to register to care for young children you will need to apply for an Enhanced Criminal Records Disclosure from the Criminal Records Bureau (CRB) for yourself and every person over the age of 16 who will be living or working on the premises.

The results of all these checks will be taken into account by Ofsted when assessing your suitability and processing your application to become a registered childminder. It is important that you complete the forms as directed and return them along with the appropriate *original* documents requested to ensure that your application is processed without delay.

Registration site visit and suitable person interview

There are three main reasons for a site visit and suitable person interview, and these are as follows:

- To enable the inspector to ensure that you are qualified and prepared to begin the task of caring for children in your home.

- To enable the inspector to satisfy themselves that your premises are safe and suitable for children to attend.

- To decide how many children you may be registered for, taking into account the space and resources you have available.

Many childminders feel apprehensive about their suitable person interview and this is understandable. It is important to remember however that the inspector is not working *against* you. Their aim is to find out whether you have the necessary aptitude to work with young children and, if they feel that improvements can be made, these will be discussed. The inspector is not looking for faults in order to refuse your registration, they are satisfying themselves that you meet the necessary criteria and will offer help and advice where necessary.

Prior to your registration site visit, which will be arranged by the inspector at a mutually convenient time, you must ensure that you are in possession of all the relevant documentation for example proof or any training and qualifications. At this stage Ofsted will usually have carried out all the necessary checks and they will already have received the appropriate references.

The inspector will use the information gathered at your interview together with the checks already made to assess whether or not you are considered a suitable person to be registered and ready to begin working as a childminder.

After conducting your interview and prior to leaving your setting, it is usual for the inspector to give you oral feedback on the outcome of the visit in order that you are clear about anything which the inspector may feel needs to be addressed prior to Ofsted granting your registration. There may be conditions imposed on you, and these may be as simple as not allowing children access to certain outside areas if they feel there is a hazard to the children, for example a pond or greenhouse. *Now* is the time to ask any questions and discuss any actions or conditions.

Action letter

In some cases, an inspector may feel that changes need to be made to your premises in order to comply with any necessary standards. Any changes deemed necessary will have been passed on to you verbally during your suitable person interview and the action letter will put these requirements in writing detailing an appropriate timescale for any work to be carried out.

Decision to register

Following a satisfactory site visit and suitable person interview, Ofsted will notify you in writing of their decision to register you as a childminder. Their decision may contain certain conditions to which you must agree to comply, and these will be outlined in the letter. At this stage you will be required to pay the registration fee and provide written acceptance of any conditions imposed on your recommendation for registration. Ofsted does not normally grant registration until the fee is paid, and a delay in sending the fee will mean a delay in issuing your registration certificate. It is an offence to begin childminding *prior* to being in receipt of your registration certificate, therefore prompt payment of the registration fee is essential.

Registration certificate

The certificate will contain your name, address and any conditions imposed with regard to your registration. This certificate is your proof of registration and must be shown to prospective parents seeking childcare. It is a condition of your registration that you display your certificate in your childminding setting when carrying out your work. If you decide to cease being a registered childminder you will be requested to return your certificate to Ofsted.

Intent to refuse registration, objection and refusal

A 'notice of intention' to refuse your application will be issued by Ofsted if they feel you do not meet all the requirements of registration. This notice will include the reasons for your refusal.

If you wish to object to Ofsted with regard to their refusal of your application you can do this by notifying them, in writing, within 14 days of receipt of your 'Intent to Refuse Registration' letter. Ofsted will assume that you do not wish to object to their decision if they have not heard from you within the 14-day period and will then issue a letter confirming the refusal in writing. At this stage your right to appeal would have to go to an independent tribunal.

Insurance

It is important that childminders understand the need for insurance and that every home-based carer is fully insured for all eventualities.

Public liability insurance is a requirement of registration and it will protect childminders against:

- Accidental death or injury to any person, including the children in your care, which may be caused by your own negligence or the activities and experiences you provide.

- Damage to other people's property by the children you are caring for.

In addition to public liability insurance you will also need to consider:

- House and contents insurance
- Car insurance.

Childminders need to be careful with regard to house and contents insurance as many insurance companies will refuse to cover childminding premises and you may need to look to a company which specializes in this type of cover. The National Childminding Association (NCMA) and Morton Michel provide specialist house and contents insurance. You can contact the NCMA by telephoning 0845 880 0044 or visiting their website www.ncma.org.uk, or Morton Michel on 0845 2570 900 or visiting their website www.mortonmichel.com.

Car insurance is not usually a problem *providing* you inform the company concerned that you use your vehicle for business purposes and let them know the nature of your business. As with many insurance policies it is always good practice to put the details of your business in writing to the insurance company to avoid any future comebacks which may prove costly to you should the insurance company refute a claim.

Employing suitable people

Childminding can at times be a lonely profession. You may find yourself at home for many hours with only very young children for company, particularly in the winter months when the weather is bad and it is not as easy to get out and about with toddlers and babies. If you have been used to working away from the home in the past, getting used to the loneliness and having the responsibility of being your own boss can be rather daunting. You must be organized to run your own business, whatever your profession, and you must take responsibility for things if they go wrong. There is no one immediately at hand to turn to for support, help and advice or to share the workload. It is for these reasons, together with friendship and companionship, that some childminders opt to work with another childminder, or to employ an assistant to work with them. There are both advantages and disadvantages of working with someone else, and we will look at some of these now.

Advantages of working with another childminder or employing an assistant

Adult company – Unless you are prepared to take the children you look after to lots of different clubs or outings, which is not always practical as these can be expensive and will have to fit in with your everyday routines, then you will find yourself spending a lot of time devoid of adult company. Being in the company of young children without any adult input affects people differently, and some childminders find it difficult.

Sharing views and ideas – Working alone can result in ideas becoming stale and unadventurous. You may have had lots of ideas for activities at the outset when starting up your business but, after a while, it can be difficult to have the motivation to come up with new ideas to stimulate the children. Having another adult present means that there is the option of 'pooling' ideas. One of you may be brilliant at artwork, while the other may have musical ability. By working together you can share your knowledge and expertise, to the benefit of the children.

Flexibility and backup – If you work alone and you or one of your own children are ill it can mean letting parents down if you are not able to go about your childminding duties. Working with another childminder or employing an assistant can help overcome this obstacle as there are always two people available. Obviously you must still adhere to the conditions of your registration and not exceed the number of children *one* of you can care for *alone*.

Reassurance – We all need reassurance sometimes and it is good to have someone there to share the trials and tribulations that running your own business can bring. There may be times when a parent is being unreasonable or is unhappy about a particular situation and it is always good to be able to seek impartial advice from someone else. It is important to remember to respect your setting's confidentiality procedures before discussing certain things with an assistant. Having someone to work with who is as keen and enthusiastic as you is a great boost and it helps to be able to motivate one another.

Emergencies – Having another adult present in times of accidents, illnesses or emergencies can be very helpful. It will be much easier to stay calm and in control of the situation if you have help readily available. By working as a team you will be able to manage any emergency situation much easier and, should a trip to the hospital be necessary, you would not have the added problem of finding someone to care for the other children you are responsible for.

Adult: child ratios increased – By working with another childminder or employing an assistant the number of children you would be registered to care for would be increased. The exact number of children will be determined by Ofsted.

Shared costs – Obviously the everyday costs of providing food and drink would not be reduced as you will probably be caring for a larger number of children if you are working with another childminder, but the cost of purchasing toys and equipment should be considerably less as you can share the cost of toys and resources.

Disadvantages of working with another childminder or assistant

Authority – It may be difficult to determine who has the overall authority when important decisions are being made. In the case of working with another childminder disputes could arise for example, depending on whose house the business is run from. If you employ an assistant you must be confident at giving clear, concise instructions and make sure the assistant is aware of exactly what is expected of them.

Differences in work attitude – Problems may arise if you and the person you are working with have very different attitudes regarding the way you wish to run the business. While one of you may be willing to improve your skills through training courses, the other may not be prepared to give up their free time in this way and resentment may arise. It must be made clear for everyone involved, prior to starting the business, what is expected from each individual.

Friendships – Friendships may suffer when two people spend long hours together day after day. You may think that you have a solid friendship but tempers can become frayed when faced with the very demanding job of caring for young children.

Working out wages, expenses, etc. – It may seem fair to split the profits of the business equally if you are working with another childminder, and likewise pay an equal proportion of the cost of purchasing toys, equipment, food and drink, but who will be responsible for calculating how much heating, lighting, gas/electricity for cooking, toilet rolls and soap are being used? Who will be expected to wash and iron the extra towels and bedding? These are all questions which need to be addressed fairly if your business is to succeed. If you employ an assistant and pay wages you will be responsible for income tax and National Insurance payments and you must be aware of, and comply with, the employment law in these cases. You will be expected to pay your employee the minimum wage, and as an employer you will also need to have employer's liability insurance in addition to public liability insurance.

Whether you decide to work alone, employ an assistant or work with another childminder is purely down to preference. What I would recommend though, if you are thinking of working with someone else is to think very carefully about what you want and how you see your business developing. Work out, in detail, how you are going to calculate your expenditure and organize your accounts. Make sure *all* parties are happy with the arrangements prior to commencing the business, and never agree to anything initially that you feel you may resent later on.

Exercise: Make a list of the factors you consider to be important when choosing a suitable assistant or co-childminder to work with. What attributes do you consider essential? How would you ensure that you chose the right person for the job?

If you do decide to employ an assistant or work with a co-childminder it is *your* responsibility to ensure that the person you choose to employ or work with is suitable for the job. In the case of a co-childminder this may be relatively easy as they will already be registered with Ofsted and therefore have undergone the relevant stringent checks all that is left for you to do is to ensure that you can work with the person and that you have a similar outlook on business matters. If you choose to employ an assistant then you must do so with caution and ensure that all the relevant checks have been made on them, and that references have been followed up *prior* to commencement of their employment.

When deciding on the suitability of employing an assistant you may find it helpful to use evidence derived from the following to help you to make up your mind:

- References – Always ask for references from the candidate's current employer and, more importantly, contact them!

- Qualifications – Ask to see the candidate's qualifications. Although holding many qualifications does not necessarily mean that a person is better suited for the job than someone with fewer awards, it does prove their willingness to learn and their competence in studying for and achieving qualifications.

- Knowledge – In addition to qualifications ask what experience and knowledge of children the candidate has.

- CRB checks – Always check that the person is suitable to work with young children.

- Identity/health checks – Make sure you are completely satisfied with who the person says they are and that they do not have a health problem which could put them or others at risk in a childminding setting.

- Employment history – Ask to see the candidate's employment history and, if they appear to have had numerous jobs, find out why.

- Interview – Use the interview to get to know the person. Ask yourself some important questions such as:

  1. Could you work with this person?

  2. Do you feel the person is capable of working on their own initiative?

  3. Is the person approachable?

  4. If there are children present, how does the person respond to them and how do they respond to the candidate?

  5. Do you feel the person would have a problem taking instructions from you?

Remember you have a duty to inform Ofsted of any changes you make to staffing, and this includes whether you decide to work with another childminder or whether you employ an assistant.

Your responsibilities to parents

Usually parents want the best for their children. How they actually go about achieving this may vary immensely. The important thing to remember is that there are many different ways of successfully bringing up children and many different factors influencing the way parents choose to do this.

Some of the more common factors which can influence the way in which parents may choose to bring up their children are listed below:

- Money and employment
- Housing
- Education
- Family structure
- Culture
- Religion.

Generally speaking, parenting styles fall into three main categories:

- Authoritarian
- Permissive
- Authoritative.

Let us now look at these styles in more detail.

Authoritarian – This type of parenting tends to be controlling. These parents have many rules in an attempt to manage the behaviour of their children. Quite often authoritarian parents have very high expectations of their children, which can often be difficult for the child to achieve.

Permissive – This tends to be the opposite of authoritarian. Permissive parents allow their children freedom of choice. Often children with permissive parents are more difficult to manage when it comes to behaviour because they have been allowed much more freedom than other children. Although choice and responsibility are good for children, it is also essential that they are not allowed an excessive amount of freedom and it should be remembered that boundaries are essential in order for children to feel safe and secure.

Authoritative – This is the category which most parents fall into. Authoritative parents attempt to manage and control their child's behaviour in a way which enables them to be easily accepted into society. They take the time to listen to their children and to explain rules and expectations.

Family structures also have an enormous effect on parenting styles and the main structures are as follows:

- The nuclear family
- The extended family
- The single-parent family
- The homosexual or lesbian family
- The reconstituted family
- The adoptive family.

Let us now look at these structures in more detail.

The nuclear family – This type of family structure consists of both parents and their children living together and sharing the responsibility of caring for their children.

The extended family – This type of family structure consists of parents, children and relatives all living close by and sometimes even in the same house and sharing the responsibility of bringing up the children. Extended family structures were traditional in this country for centuries and are still common practice in many parts of the world.

The single-parent family – This type of family structure consists of one parent living on their own with their children. This type of family occurs when the parents have divorced or separated, when one parent has died or when a woman has actively chosen to have a child without the support of the father.

The homosexual/lesbian family – This type of family structure consists of one natural parent living with a partner of the same sex, along with their children.

The reconstituted family – This type of family structure consists of one natural parent and one step-parent living together with the children.

The adoptive family – This type of family structure consists of a child who is not living with one or both of their natural parents. Sometimes the child may be unaware that they are adopted and therefore appear to be part of a *nuclear* family structure.

Parents and indeed, their children, require different things from childcare and it is the responsibility of the childminder to accommodate their wishes as much as possible. Influencing factors could well be the age and stage of development of the child. Generally speaking parents are looking for childcare which offers their child the chance to be in a stimulating, safe environment. Additional factors they may be looking for are:

- A loving, caring environment
- A chance for their child to mix with other children
- A chance to build on their child's confidence
- A start to the child's education
- A variety of experiences
- An established routine which their child can relate to.

It is probably true to say that most parents looking for childcare are interested in the safety of the environment and the opportunities and experiences the childminder can offer their child. Safety is a very important part of a childminder's job and you have a responsibility to ensure that the children in your care are safe at all times. In order to do this it is essential that you look closely at all the indoor and outdoor areas you use for your childminding business and scrutinize every aspect of safety. Pay special attention to:

- Equipment – make regular checks to ensure that there are no worn or broken parts, and replace or repair when necessary.
- Toys – make regular checks to ensure that there are no missing or broken parts, and replace or repair when necessary.
- Dangerous items – think carefully about how you store knives, medicines, matches, cleaning fluids, alcohol, plastic bags, etc.
- Electrical items – fit locks to fridges, freezers, washing machines, etc. and ensure that flexes from toasters, irons and kettles are not left trailing over work surfaces.
- Stair gates – these should be fitted to both the top and the bottom of the stairs.

- Fires – guards should be securely fitted around the whole of the fire and its surround.

- Radiators – ensure that these are not too hot when touched and, if necessary, fit covers on them.

- Electrical sockets – these should be covered.

- Food – it is essential that you practise safe and hygienic work methods when storing, preparing and cooking food.

- Pets – ensure that pets are not allowed on tables or work surfaces and that their feeding bowls, toys, litter trays, etc. are not accessible to children. Pets should be routinely vaccinated and treated appropriately for worms and fleas.

- Smoke alarms – should be fitted and working, check batteries regularly.

- Fire blanket/extinguisher – should be in good working order and easily accessible.

- Nappies – hygienic practices must be followed with regard to the changing and disposing of nappies.

- Bedding/towels – each child should be provided with their own clean bedding, towels, flannels or sponges.

- Low-level glass – ensure that glass in windows, doors, coffee tables, greenhouses, etc. conforms to safety standards.

- Windows – should be fitted with safety catches and no furniture should be placed directly underneath which children can climb on.

- Banisters/railings – check that these are safe and secure and that they do not have spaces where a child could trap their hands, feet or head.

- Tablecloths – ensure that these are not left trailing.

- Rugs/carpets – ensure that no one can trip over rugs or worn/frayed carpets.

- Gardens – children must not be allowed access to ponds, water butts, sheds, greenhouses, streams, wells, pools, fountains, garages, etc. Poisonous plants must be removed from the garden area accessible to the children and gates and fences must be checked regularly to ensure they are secure. All dangerous items such as garden equipment must be securely locked away and outdoor toys and equipment must be checked regularly for signs of wear and tear. Pets must not be exercised in the garden area used for childminding purposes.

Exercise: Carry out a detailed survey of your home and garden and make a list of any potential hazards you uncover. Critically examine the dangers you discover and describe how you can eliminate these potential hazards.

Parents who chose a childminder over a nursery setting for their child will do so for a number of reasons. Although some nurseries offer excellent opportunities for children, childminders come into their own for several reasons as they can offer children:

- Smaller groups – most childminders are registered to care for three children under the age of 5 and can therefore offer a much more personal service.

- The same carer – as with small groups, being cared for by the same person every day has many benefits for a child and is preferable over having to get used to several carers in a nursery setting. This can be particularly beneficial to a child who finds new situations difficult to handle.

- Continuity of care – childminders often care for children from several weeks old right through their school years. This is something that nurseries cannot offer and alternative childcare often has to be found once a child begins school.

- Childminders often become an extension of the child's family as excellent friendships may be forged.

- Childminders have a better knowledge and understanding of the children as they are usually the only people, other than the child's parents, who are caring for the child and they are therefore in an excellent position to spot any changes in behaviour, etc. early on.

Today's working parents lead busy, stressful lives and, although it is true to say that most childminders also lead hectic lives and work long hours, this is often forgotten when a problem arises as people tend to see things only from their own point of view. When dealing with any type of complaint it is important to remember to:

- Stay calm

- Listen to what the parents have to say

- Do not interrupt when someone else is telling you something

- Get your own message across without resorting to apportioning blame

- Refrain from shouting or becoming aggressive.

Problems can and will occur from time to time, however it is important to remember that, although not accepting the blame for every little thing that may go wrong, you are responsible for ensuring the smooth running of your business, and dealing with any complaints effectively is all part of your job. It is true to say that some parents can be unreasonable, but by writing and maintaining appropriate contracts and policies you should be well on the way to eliminating many of the common problems immediately. Childminding is a *partnership* and it is up to you to ensure that this partnership runs smoothly.

Many of the problems which usually occur are due to misunderstandings, and this is where a watertight contract comes into its own (for more about contracts see Chapter 7). Always take the time to word your contracts accurately and explain them to parents before inviting them to sign. Make sure that they fully understand what is expected of them and what they in return can expect from you.

Your policies and procedures also go a long way to ensuring that misunderstandings do not occur, and you should think carefully about what you are asking of the parents and their children (for more about policies see Chapter 7).

Common problems

Behaviour – Often your own rules regarding behaviour may differ from those of the child's parents. However, it is important to remember that rules have to be made and kept in order for all the children in your setting to be happy and enjoy their time with you, and it must be made clear that you expect all the children to abide by your rules *regardless* of what they are allowed to do at home.

Payment – Problems can sometimes arise when parents become lax with their payments and fail to pay on time. These problems can easily be rectified by reminding parents of the contract you have with them and, if necessary, incorporating an additional fee into the contract for late payment. You will find that parents are unhappy paying extra and will ensure that they pay on time once you have exercised your rights to a late-payment fee.

Dietary requirements – Ideally these issues will be discussed and agreed early on, before the child takes up a place with you. You must always seek the preference of parents where sweets, sugary snacks and fizzy drinks are concerned. Arguably these should be kept to a minimum regardless of parental preference; but you must never give a child any of these if their parents have specifically requested you not to.

Holidays – Like payments, this should be discussed and agreed prior to signing the contract. Often parents who have been happy to accept that you will have five weeks' holiday a year are less quick to accept this if your dates are different to theirs and they need to find alternative cover for the time you are away. This problem can be avoided by liaising with the parents about holiday dates and, where possible, give them lots of notice or plan your holidays together so that your dates coincide.

No matter how hard you work, how many hours you devote to your business, or how dedicated you are to your job, there are very few childminders who will not, at some point in their careers, come across a problem or receive a complaint. This is because all families are unique and will not agree with everything you do and say all of the time. As the saying goes, you *'cannot please all of the people all of the time'*, but you should be striving to *'please most of the people most of the time'*. If you take the time to listen to parents and accept that everyone is different, and that they have different opinions and values then you will be well on the way to dealing with any potential problems should they arise.

If you are unfortunate enough to receive a complaint, try to resolve the problem as amicably as possible. This is necessary both from a business point of view and from the child's point of view. Children can very quickly detect any animosity between their parents and their childminder and they will become upset and confused if their main carers are at loggerheads.

Encourage parents to meet with you, after work hours when interruptions are at a minimum, to discuss the problem. Allow them to put their point of view across, listen to them without interrupting and take on board what they are saying. After they have had their say, put your own point of view across in a calm and reasonable manner. Do not blame anyone; accept that there has been a difference of opinion and seek to resolve the matter.

When you are communicating with parents it is essential that you treat them as equals. Although it is important to get your own message across it is equally important to listen to, value and respect the views of the parents in order to establish a friendly relationship based on trust and mutual understanding. A poor relationship with the child's parents will inevitably cause problems in the long run.

Your responsibilities to children

Unlike parents, children are relatively easy to keep happy! They will not make any unreasonable demands on you and will not expect you to perform miracles. Children are usually happy and content if they feel safe, valued and are offered appropriate activities to stimulate their minds. It is of course your duty as a childminder to enhance this and encourage them to achieve their full potential and ensure that they are loved, welcomed and valued.

In order for Ofsted to make their judgement about the overall quality of your childminding setting the inspector will ask the very important question: *What is it like for a child here?* The inspector will judge how well you meet a series of outcomes for children, these outcomes are as follows:

- How do you help children to be healthy?

- How do you protect children from harm or neglect and help them to stay safe?

- How do you help children to enjoy themselves and achieve their full potential?

- How do you help children to make a positive contribution to your setting and to the wider community?

- How do you help children to achieve economic well-being?

Children's rights

The United Nations Convention on the Rights of the Child applies to everyone under the age of 18 years and consists of 54 agreed articles. Almost every country in the world has agreed to and signed this very important treaty, underlying its importance. There are certain Acts of Parliament which exist and are in place to promote the equality of opportunity and to prevent discrimination. The Acts include the Children Act 1989 which requires that the regulatory body has a set of policies in practice for equality of opportunity and that these policies are reviewed regularly. All childcare practitioners should receive regular updates relating to equal opportunities and they should be provided with details of any relevant training as and when necessary.

The Children Act 1989 acknowledges the importance of the child's wishes and opinions. The Act emphasizes the need for parents and carers to be *responsible* for their children rather than to have *rights over* them.

Children have five basic needs. These needs are illustrated in the diagram below.

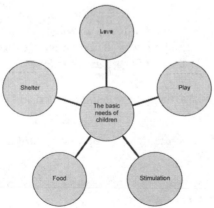

Fig 2.2   *The basic needs of children*

The basic human rights of children entitle them to things such as food, health care and protection from abuse. However, a child's rights are different from those of an adult as children cannot always stand up for themselves. Children need a special set of rights which take into account their vulnerability and which ensure that adults take responsibility for their protection, stimulation and development. The UN Convention on the Rights of the Child outlines the basic human rights of *all* children *everywhere*.

All children have the right to:

- Survival
- Protection from harm, abuse and exploitation
- Develop to their full potential
- Participate fully in social, cultural and family life
- Express their views
- Have their views listened to, valued and taken into account
- Play, rest and enjoy their lives.

There are certain rights outlined in the UN Convention which relate particularly to childcare and education, and it is these rights of the child that childminders should be most concerned with. The rights which affect childcare are as follows:

- Children have the right to sufficient food and clean water for their needs
- Children have the right to appropriate health care and medicines
- Children have the right to be with their family or those who will care for them best
- Children have the right to play

- Children have the right to be safe and free from harm and neglect

- Children have the right to free education

- Children should not be exploited as cheap labour or soldiers

- Children have the right to an adequate standard of living

- Disabled children have the right to special care and training.

It is probably true to say that the most difficult time for a childminder to keep a child happy is when the child is new to the setting and is missing their parents. This is particularly true for a young child who has been with their mother from birth and who may now need a childminder in order for their mother to return to work. You will not be able to take the place of the child's mother, while they are in your setting, and you should not be striving to do this. It is your job to reassure the child, offer appropriate activities and comfort them when they are upset. You will have to adjust your usual routine to cater for the new child and to offer additional support until they have settled into your setting.

In some ways it is easier to settle a young baby into your setting than an older child. However, babies, when they get to the age of around eight months, start to become aware of strangers and may well go through a phase of 'missing mummy or daddy'. Babies of this age can often become upset when being left and you would be wise to prepare the parents for this possibility. Likewise the parents of the child may be very likely to miss their baby and may also need your support and reassurance.

Ideally before a child starts their placement with you, you will have had the opportunity to meet them on several occasions. You may decide to arrange to visit them in their own home and to get to know them on 'familiar territory', or you may prefer to arrange short visits at your own house so that the child can get used to their new setting. You may even decide on a mixture of both. It is important to discuss with the parents which strategy they feel will work best for their child.

Prior to a baby or child starting in your care you will need to gather as much information about them from their parents as possible in order to prepare yourself for the task ahead. The more information you have about a child, their likes, dislikes, fears and anxieties, the more equipped you will be to deal with any scenarios thrown at you.

It is important to remember that parents may feel equally, if not more, anxious than their child. They may have feelings of guilt about leaving their child. Reassure them that these feelings are all perfectly normal and offer them the support they need.

Tips for settling children into your childminding setting

- Arrange short visits, prior to the placement commencing, in order to allow the child time to get to know their surroundings.

- Encourage parents to stay with their child for a while, particularly during the first few days, if this is possible.

- Offer support and encouragement to both the child and their parents.

- Encourage the child to bring a special toy or comforter from home.

- Avoid forcing the child to join in activities or games. If they prefer to sit and watch for a while, allow them to do this and to mix only when they are ready.

- Offer cuddles and reassurance if the child becomes distressed, remember to allow the child to take the lead on this level and never force a child to sit with you and be cuddled if they do not want to do so.

- Offer simple, straightforward activities immediately after their parent has left, to take their mind off the separation. Ideally you will have discovered what particular activities the child prefers and you will be able to offer these. Avoid anything which requires a lot of concentration.

Once a parent has decided they are going, encourage them to do just that! Long, drawn-out goodbyes are not a good idea, and can be stressful for everyone. Encourage the parents to establish a routine for saying goodbye and to stick to it. Children may become very upset if the departure is delayed, and a child who is not crying at the start of the farewell may well be hysterical by the time it has finished! Always encourage the parent to actually say goodbye and kiss the child. Never allow them to 'sneak' off without telling their child they are going. This may result in the child becoming clingy as they will come to expect their parent to 'disappear'. If a child does not understand where their parent has gone they may suffer unnecessary distress and become distrustful.

Below is a routine which you may like to encourage parents to follow when saying goodbye to their child, particularly in the early stages of the placement when the child is still settling in.

- Parent and child arrive at your house

- Greet both the parent and child warmly as they come in

- Either you or the parent takes the child's coat off

- Ideally, in the case of an older child, you will already have a suitable activity prepared and you should then tell them about it

- Prior to the child commencing the activity, encourage them to kiss their parent and say goodbye

- Encourage the parent to tell their child that they are going and that they will be back at lunchtime/teatime

- Allow the parent and child to say goodbye in their own way

- Parent leaves.

Chapter Three

Your Inspection

The inspector – friend or foe?

Many childminders and indeed schoolteachers dread their routine inspection by Ofsted. Having an Ofsted inspector or inspectors come into your home to assess and grade the work you do can be nerve-wracking even for experienced, confident childminders who have dozens of qualifications and are at the top of their profession, therefore it is understandable that childminders with only a few years experience and limited training may feel out of their depth when their inspection is looming. The important thing to remember is that the inspector is *not your enemy!* Armed with a laptop and endless questions, you may feel the inspector is here to interrogate and reprimand but the opposite is actually the case. The inspector, like yourself, has a job to do and their job is to provide regular checks to ensure that all registered childminders are continuing to meet appropriate standards of day care. The inspector should not be regarded as someone out to 'trip you up' or 'catch you out', and these negative feelings will only leave you feeling more ill at ease if you allow them to surface.

If you are following the recommended procedures for childminding and are up to date with all your essential paperwork (for more on this see Chapter 7) then you should have nothing to worry about and only a little preparation by you for the inspection should be required.

What to expect from your inspection

Registration and inspections used to be carried out by the local authority, however in 2001 this was transferred to the Ofsted directorate. It is the job of Ofsted inspectors to look at, and monitor, the ways in which childcare providers demonstrate how they meet the necessary criteria.

The Childcare Act 2006 has brought about new changes as it sets out how early years provision must be registered, and introduces the EYFS as the statutory framework for the education and welfare of children from birth to the 31 August following their fifth birthday.

From September 2008 the EYFS has formed the basis of inspections of provision for young children and the introduction of this framework allows Ofsted the opportunity of bringing greater consistency to the inspection of early years provision across the sector.

Ofsted have the power to investigate your childminding setting to ensure that you are meeting the appropriate criteria and can request that changes are made if necessary. Ofsted also have the power to terminate your registration if your setting does not conform to the appropriate criteria.

Newly registered childminders will usually have their first Ofsted inspection within a short period of time after their registration. After the initial inspection Ofsted will usually carry out further inspections at least once every three years. However in certain circumstances, as listed below, inspections will be more frequent.

- If the last inspection concluded that the quality of childcare you provide had significant weaknesses.

- If there have been significant changes to the setting since the last inspection, such as a change of premises.

- If a complaint has been made against you that suggests you are not meeting the appropriate criteria or providing adequate care for the children.

Ofsted want to see your setting running as normally as possible on any given day without you having to make any special arrangements. However, they also realize that many childminders spend a large amount of their time out of the home either on school runs, attending support groups, toddler sessions, etc. and therefore, to avoid calling when you may not be at home, the inspector will usually telephone a few days in advance to check whether there are any days in the coming week when it would not be suitable for someone to visit.

First of all, it is natural to feel a little nervous about your inspection, particularly if you are a newly qualified childminder and have had little or no experience in dealing with childcare inspections. Even those of us who have been childminding for many years still feel a little apprehensive about the inspection; after all someone is coming into your home to inspect and grade a service you are providing, and you will be striving to achieve the best grading possible – outstanding!

When an inspector arrives at your home, check their ID *before* allowing them access! This will not antagonize the inspector, moreover it will show that you are sincere about the safety of the children in your care and that you are aware of the correct procedure regarding access to strangers while carrying out your childminding duties. If the inspector cannot show you any ID, or you are in any doubt whatsoever about who they say they are, then leave them on the doorstep while you clarify the situation with your Ofsted regional office.

It is important to carry on your normal routine without making any changes. Disruption should be kept to a minimum although, of course, you will need to be available to talk with the inspector when required. Initially you will be informed of how the inspection will be carried out, and this is usually as follows:

- The inspector will observe what the children and adults in the setting are doing.

- The inspector will talk to the children and, if possible, the parents to find out their views on the childcare provided. It is a good idea to request some or all of the parents to complete questionnaires prior to your inspection, giving their ideas and opinions of the service you provide if they cannot be present in person during the inspection, this will enable the inspector to have an idea of how your service is viewed by the parents of the children you care for.

- The inspector will check your premises and equipment to ensure that they are safe and suitable and check how well they are used to promote outcomes for children.

- The inspector will check your written records, procedures and any other necessary documentation.

Throughout the inspection the inspector will make notes of their findings. When the inspection is complete, usually after about two hours, the inspector will let you know the outcome of their findings. You will normally see a display of the inspector's judgements on a laptop computer and it is these judgements which will be included in your final report. At this point you may correct factual information or ask for further clarification of any of the points the inspector raises.

After your inspection you will be sent an inspection report. If there are any factual errors in the report at this stage you must inform Ofsted immediately as the report will be published on the internet shortly after. The report, when published on the internet, will not include your name or your full address.

If your childcare provision is judged as satisfactory or good, the report will include recommendations to help you to improve your provision further. The inspector will check whether these recommendations have been implemented at your next inspection (within three years from the date of your last inspection). However if the inspector considers that the quality of care you are providing is inadequate, then it will be because you are failing to meet the necessary criteria. If this judgement is made Ofsted will either:

- Send you a letter to tell you what action you must take to improve the care you provide. This letter is called a *notice of action to improve*. You will be required to let Ofsted know when you have taken the necessary action, and you may receive an announced or unannounced visit to check that the necessary improvements have been made. If you ignore the notice of action or the improvements you make have little impact on the outcome of your childcare provision then Ofsted may take further enforcement measures. You will receive a further inspection within six to 12 months of your initial visit.

- If your childcare provision is classed as poor and is considered in need of immediate improvement then Ofsted will take enforcement action such as issuing you with a *compliance notice*. An inspector will follow this notice up to ensure that the improvements have been made. In rare cases Ofsted may consider *suspending* or *cancelling* your registration. If Ofsted consider it necessary to take serious action against your setting, but still allow your registration to continue, then they will inspect your premises again either at the date given on any enforcement action or within three to six months, whichever is the sooner.

How to impress the inspector

Preparation is a key factor when anticipating your forthcoming inspection. No one can accurately guess exactly what will happen during an inspection. This will depend entirely on the day the inspection takes place, which children you are caring for at the time, even how the children are feeling on that particular day can have an impact on the way your inspection may go. If one of the children in your care is feeling a bit off colour or tired, or simply refusing to cooperate, it may add to the stress you are already feeling. The important thing to remember is that the inspector understands that children rarely do exactly what they are expected to and it is how you *handle* any awkward or difficult situations that will be looked at. Try to relax and act as normally as possible. Go about your daily routines as you usually would and avoid making changes that would confuse or disrupt the children's usual patterns. After all, if you are complying with the requirements set out by Ofsted and are working within the set criteria *all of the time*, which is what you should be doing, then you really have little to worry about.

Although you will be striving to achieve an 'outstanding' grade for your business it is important to remember that the inspector is looking at how you run your business *all* of the time and not just for the hours they are present, therefore striving to overly impress is unnecessary and will come across as false.

Taking the inspector on a brief tour of your premises and pointing out how you have made each of the areas safe, hygienic and suitable for the children will help you to answer many of the questions the inspector will inevitably raise and you will be able to elaborate on the facilities you have available.

Think carefully about each of the important points the inspector may ask and use each area of your premises to satisfy them that you are aware of, and concerned with, the aspects in question. For example:

- Hygienic work practices could be discussed when showing the inspector your bathroom, toilet and nappy-changing facilities.

- Safety could be discussed in the playroom and outdoor areas.

- Dietary needs, hygiene and healthy eating could be discussed in the kitchen.

- Learning and development could be discussed when showing the inspector the activities, resources and experiences you provide.

These are just a few of the many ways you can provide evidence of your working practice.

There are a number of other points which you should consider to ensure that you are ready for your inspection and these are listed below:

- Ensure that you and any assistants or other childminders you work with are familiar with all the relevant documents needed for running a childminding business, for example the EYFS framework.

- Ensure that you have put right any weaknesses identified in your last inspection report, if applicable.

- Ensure that you have completed the self-evaluation form.

- Ensure that you have all the required records which the inspector will need to see such as contracts, attendance register, etc.

- Keep any information about how parents view your service

and any improvements you have made as a result. It is a good idea to produce a simple questionnaire to give to parents, prior to your inspection or periodically, say once a year, to establish how the parents of the children you care for view your setting and the childcare provision you provide. Often constructive criticism can be very helpful and we all respond well to praise! (An example of a questionnaire you could adapt to suit your own setting is shown below.)

- Ensure that you have available any records you keep of complaints about the childcare you provide.

- Ensure that you have notified Ofsted of any significant changes you have made to your provision for example any changes to the premises or people employed to look after the children.

QUESTIONNAIRE FOR PARENTS

In order that I can continue to provide a good quality childcare service that benefits all the children and their parents I would be much obliged if you would kindly take the time to complete this short questionnaire and return it to me as soon as possible.

1. Are you happy with the overall childcare I provide for your child/children?

2. If there are any improvements you feel I could make which would be of benefit to you what would these be?

3. Are the hours I am available to work acceptable to you?

4. Are you happy with the meals I provide? Do you have any suggestions for improvements?

5. Are you happy with the activities I provide for your

> child/children? Do you think these could be improved in any way?
>
> 6. Do you consider that your child is happy in my setting and are there any ways I could make their time with me more enjoyable?
>
> 7. If your child/children are of school age do you consider that they get sufficient help from me with regard to their homework/studies? Can you suggest any improvement?
>
> 8. Are you happy with the information I provide with regard to your child's daily routines? Is there any further information you would like?
>
> 9. Are there any further comments you would like to make which may help me to continually strive to improve my day care and before/after school service in order that all the children in my care remain happy and secure?

This questionnaire can be adapted to suit your own childcare setting and it may be a good idea to distribute these periodically, especially if you have got new children starting. A good time to give a questionnaire out may be just prior to renewing a contract so that any changes implemented can be reflected on the contract and you can be sure that the service you provide is the right one for the family.

Exercise: Create your own questionnaire to give to parents. Remember to include all important aspects of the child's care and encourage the parents to add their own views and ideas by asking 'open ended' questions rather than those that require a simple yes/no answer.

Self-evaluation is well established in schools where they are encouraged to record regularly the outcomes of their self-evaluation on a SEF (schools) which Ofsted enables them to access, complete and submit online.

In September 2008 Ofsted introduced a similar emphasis on self-improvement to inspections of all types of early years settings, including childminders. Early years settings are able to complete and submit the SEF online which can then be regularly updated when changes occur. Completed, up-to-date SEFs also contribute to the inspection process. They should enable inspectors to plan inspections based on those aspects of early years provision that practitioners consider work well along with those they are seeking to improve.

Ofsted will issue all childminders with a self-evaluation form prior to their planned inspection. The form sets out a series of questions and asks the childminder to grade themselves on the same scale as the inspector uses i.e., Grade 1 Outstanding, Grade 2 Good, Grade 3 Satisfactory and Grade 4 Inadequate. The self-evaluation form also lists the necessary documents you must have available to show the inspector during your inspection. These documents include:

- The child's personal details including their full name, address, date of birth, emergency contact numbers, medical history, etc.

- The parent's personal details including their full name/s, address/es and contact details.

- Accident and medical records.

- Attendance register.

Although not a compulsory requirement of Ofsted you may also like to develop various policies (for more about these see Chapter

7) and a leaflet, newsletter, welcome pack and portfolio setting out details of the service you provide, and of course you should show all of these to the inspector.

Keeping the children entertained during your inspection

It has to be said that the children themselves will have a lot to do with the way your inspection goes! If you are caring for a child who often resorts to temper tantrums, sulks or has difficulty cooperating then don't make the mistake of thinking that they will be on their best behaviour because there is a stranger present – this will simply not happen! In fact often the reverse may be true as they strive to push the boundaries even further to see if they can get away with anything more while someone new is in the setting.

The key here is to be prepared. Unless you have only just begun to care for a child then you should have a good idea of what makes them 'tick', their likes and dislikes, what triggers unacceptable behaviour, etc., and it is paramount that you are prepared for all eventualities. One of the reasons why you should not change your usual routine is so that you don't upset or confuse children who rely on the daily structure for security. Therefore if you usually serve a snack at 10 a.m., do not put this off because the inspector is present – rest assured most children will ask for it! If a child usually has a nap at a set time then make sure you keep to this routine to avoid the child becoming over tired which often results in unacceptable behaviour which will, of course, add to your problems.

It is important to focus on the aspects which are important during your inspection and this does *not* include entertaining the inspector! Your job is to care for the children. Although you will be expected to provide information and answer questions, this has to be done *while* you are carrying out your duties and not *instead* of them.

Be aware, at all times, how the children are behaving and how they are responding to the activities you have provided. You should have a good idea of the level of concentration the children have and the stage of development they are at and it is unrealistic to expect a 2 year old to sit at a table with a jigsaw puzzle for two hours while you give the inspector a tour of your home.

Change the activities you provide regularly and, immediately the children appear bored or distracted, introduce something new for them to do. Your experience of caring for children should help you to know which activities are enjoyed the most by the children and often painting, play-dough modelling, junk modelling and stories are effective.

Planning is a vital part of a childminder's job and never has this been more evident than during inspections. If you plan your work effectively a visit from an inspector should not throw your day into chaos as you should already know what you are hoping to do with the children during that particular day, and should not therefore be frantically scouring the cupboard for a bald paint brush or dried-out play dough – this is a sure sign that your daily activities are unplanned or even non-existent, and may lead the inspector to believe that you provide little opportunity for the children to play and learn.

Exercise: Focus on the children who are presently in your care and make a list of the activities and toys they enjoy engaging with. If an inspector arrived at your home tomorrow to carry out an inspection, would you have adequate resources to keep the children happy and entertained? If your answer to this question is 'no' you need to seriously evaluate your practice. Children need to be adequately entertained and engaged in exciting and interesting learning activities and experiences *every* day!

Chapter Four
Early Years Foundation Stage

What the Early Years Foundation Stage means to childminders

The Early Years Foundation Stage came into force from September 2008. This document brings together the three previous documents which were currently used by practitioners working with young children:

- The National Standards for Under 8s in Day Care and Childminding

- The Birth to Three Framework, and

- The Curriculum Guidance for the Foundation Stage.

A new system for inspection was introduced for day care settings to ensure that children were protected from harm and allowed the support they needed to reach their full potential. Children and young people across the country were consulted about what matters the most to them and the following five *Every Child Matters* outcomes were the result of this consultation:

- Being healthy

- Staying safe

- Enjoying and achieving

- Making a positive contribution

- Economic well-being.

In 2006, the Childcare Act came into force. The Act has four parts:

- Duties on local authorities in England

- Duties on local authorities in Wales

- Regulation and inspection arrangements for childcare providers in England

- General provisions.

The Act takes forward the four key themes from the Ten Year Childcare Strategy (2004), these four themes being:

- Allowing parents choice and flexibility with regard to balancing work and family life.

- Availability of high quality, flexible childcare places for all families with children aged up to 14 years.

- High quality provision incorporating highly skilled childcare and early years practitioners.

- Affordability for flexible, high quality childcare which is appropriate to the needs of each individual child.

The Childcare Act requires all local authorities to improve the outcomes for children up to the age of 5 years.

From September 2008 childcare providers began being inspected by Ofsted under sections 49 and 50 of the Childcare Act 2006. Providers who were registered with Ofsted prior to September 2008 will have been transferred to the Early Years Register (EYR). The Childcare Register has two parts:

- Compulsory (as from September 2008)

- Voluntary (as from April 2007).

The compulsory part of the register is for providers who offer care for children up to the age of 8 years and the voluntary part is for providers who previously were unable to register with Ofsted, i.e. providers such as nannies, childminders who only care for children over the age of 8 years, holiday clubs, etc.

The Early Years Foundation Stage pack

Every childminder should be in receipt of an Early Years Foundation Stage pack. The pack consists of the following resources to help practitioners incorporate the EYFS into their practice:

- Statutory framework
- Practice guidance
- CD-ROM
- Poster
- Principles into practice cards.

From September 2008 the EYFS became mandatory for all schools and early years providers in Ofsted registered settings. The main elements of the EYFS are:

- Welfare requirements
- Learning and development requirements.

The welfare requirements consist of:

- Safeguarding and promoting children's welfare
- Suitable people

- Suitable premises, environments and equipment
- Organization
- Documentation.

The learning and development requirements consist of six areas:

- Personal, Social and Emotional Development
- Communication, Language and Literacy
- Problem Solving, Reasoning and Numeracy
- Knowledge and Understanding of the World
- Physical Development
- Creative Development.

Those practitioners who previously worked using the 14 National Standards of Care for Under 8s in Day Care and Childminding should be able to recognize these standards within the requirements listed above, for example Standard One was previously 'suitable person' and Standard Two was previously 'organization'.

Every registered childcare setting has a duty to ensure that their provision meets all the necessary criteria of the EYFS just as they were previously bound by the national standards.

By using the poster inside the EYFS pack you have a starting point from which to work. The poster clearly identifies the *four themes*:

- A unique child
- Positive relationships
- Enabling environments
- Learning and development.

The poster also highlights the *four principles*:

- Every child is a competent learner from birth who can be resilient, capable, confident and self-assured.

- Children learn to be strong and independent from a base of loving and secure relationships with parents and/or a key person.

- The environment plays a key role in supporting and extending children's development and learning.

- Children learn and develop in different ways and at different rates, and all areas of learning and development are equally important and inter-connected.

Finally, the poster identifies the *16 commitments*:

- Child development
- Inclusive practice
- Keeping safe
- Health and well-being
- Respecting each other
- Parents as partners
- Supporting learning
- Key person
- Observation, assessment and planning
- Supporting every child
- The learning environment
- The wider context
- Play and exploration

- Active learning
- Creativity and critical thinking
- Six areas of learning and development.

Producing evidence to support your practice of the Early Years Foundation Stage

It is all well and good being in possession of the EYFS pack with its colourful cards and glossy poster, but what exactly needs to be done with it? Producing evidence to show that you are committed to the framework is where the work begins!

So, what exactly do the five *Every Child Matters* outcomes mean and how can childminders implement them?

Being healthy – This requires the childminder to ensure that the children in their care enjoy good physical and mental health and that they are encouraged to take part in regular exercise and live a healthy lifestyle.

Staying safe – This requires the childminder to ensure that the children in their care are protected from harm and neglect.

Enjoying and achieving – This requires the childminder to ensure that the children in their care are encouraged to develop appropriate skills for use in later life and to get the most from the activities and experiences they participate in.

Making a positive contribution – This requires the childminder to ensure that the children in their care are encouraged to become involved in the community and that they learn how to behave in a social and responsible manner.

Economic well-being – This requires the childminder to ensure that the children in their care are not prevented from achieving their full potential in life through economic disadvantage.

Exercise: Look closely at the five *Every Child Matters* outcomes and make a list of the activities, resources and experiences you feel you could provide for children in your setting in order for them to achieve these five outcomes.

For childminders to be in a position to support children in order for them to reach these five outcomes it is vital that they understand how babies and children develop so that they can plan appropriate activities and learning opportunities. Every child is *unique* and will develop at varying rates. Child development and learning can be broken down into six categories, all of which are equally important. If we look at these six areas in more depth we can see how childminders can provide the children in their care with experiences and the support they need to reach their full potential in each of these areas.

Personal, Social and Emotional Development – this involves:

- Looking at the child's dispositions and attitudes
- Building on the child's confidence and encouraging self-esteem
- Supporting the child when developing relationships
- Promoting positive behaviour and self-control
- Encouraging the child to learn self-care skills
- Encouraging a sense of community.

When promoting this aspect of a child's learning and

development childminders need to consider a number of things including:

1. How they provide the child with a positive role model.

2. How they promote learning opportunities to explore religious beliefs and cultural backgrounds.

3. How the child is encouraged to play both alone and as part of a group.

4. How the childminder ensures that they form loving relationships with the children in their care and takes the time to listen to and value the child's contribution.

5. How the child is encouraged to follow their own interests.

Communication, Language and Literacy – this involves:

- Language for communication
- Language for thinking
- Linking sounds and letters
- Reading
- Writing
- Handwriting.

When promoting this aspect of a child's learning and development childminders need to consider a number of things including:

1. How they incorporate opportunities to read books, recite nursery rhymes, sing songs, etc., into their daily routines.

2. How they encourage the child to communicate with adults and children in the setting by conveying their thoughts, ideas and suggestions.

3. How feelings and emotions are explored.

4. How children who are learning English as a second language are encouraged to explore their home language, in addition to English and how parents and other professionals are involved.

5. How ICT is used in the setting.

Problem Solving, Reasoning and Numeracy – this involves:

- Encouraging the child to use numbers as labels and for counting

- Involving the child in calculations

- Including opportunities to explore shape, space and measurement.

When promoting this aspect of a child's learning and development, childminders need to consider a number of things including:

1. Encouraging the child to ask questions, explore concepts and discover things for themselves.

2. Allowing sufficient time for the child to complete tasks and develop ideas of their own.

3. Offering encouragement for the child to explore real-life problems such as counting, pairing up, matching, etc.

Knowledge and Understanding of the World – this involves:

- Giving the child opportunities to explore and investigate

- Providing resources for designing and making

- Promoting ICT

- Exploring the concepts of time, place and communities.

When promoting this aspect of a child's learning and development childminders need to consider a number of things including:

1. Encouraging the child to explore and acknowledge the differences in issues such as religion, disability, special educational needs, gender, ethnicity, language, etc.

2. Offering a stimulating environment with engaging activities and experiences to hold the child's interest and imagination.

3. Involving parents in order to extend the child's knowledge and experiences.

Physical Development – this involves:

- Encouraging the child to explore movement and space
- Promoting health and body awareness
- Offering opportunities to use equipment and materials.

When promoting this aspect of a child's learning and development childminders need to consider a number of things including:

1. Encouraging the child to explore movement such as climbing and balancing.

2. Promoting awareness of healthy exercise.

3. Offering opportunities for the child to take part in activities which will develop their skills of movement.

4. Ensuring that the provision is inclusive with additional support available for those who may need it.

Creative Development – this involves:

- Offering opportunities for the child to be creative by allowing them to respond to experiences and express their own ideas.

- Encouraging the child to take part in music and dance.

- Encouraging the child to use and develop their imagination through play.

- Providing opportunities for the child to explore media and materials.

When promoting this aspect of a child's learning and development childminders need to consider a number of things including:

1. Showing children that you value their ideas.

2. Offering a range of materials and resources from a variety of cultures to encourage different ideas.

3. Showing children that it is the 'process' rather than the 'finished product' which is important.

The above lists are far from exhaustive and experienced childminders should be able to think of many ways in which they can promote children's learning within these six areas and extend the child's knowledge.

Exercise: Look again at the six areas of learning and development and try to think of ways in which you could extend the lists given above.

It is important, when considering which activities and experiences to provide, that you take into account the ages and stages of development of each of the children in your care and their interests. It is equally important that the activities and experiences extend to the outdoor environment in addition to indoors.

Childminders need to keep in mind that development is a continual process in which the child's body, brain and behaviour will become more complex. It is important for practitioners to focus on the fact that all children are competent learners. They can be resilient, capable, confident and self-assured.

Child development involves the studying of patterns of growth and achievements from which guidelines are drawn up. These guidelines effectively cover what is considered to be the 'normal' patterns of child development which are generally known as 'milestones'. Developmental milestones are, however, simply indicators of the general trends in development in children across the globe and these findings should be looked at for general guidance only. It is important to remember that all children are unique, they will develop and grow at their own rate and practitioners need to understand the importance of looking not just at each individual aspect of a child's development but, more importantly, at the child as a whole.

Although children develop and grow at different speeds they will, unless they have some form of disability, develop and grow in the same way. That is to say that all children will learn to sit before they can stand, stand before they can walk and walk before they can run.

Chapter Five

Achieving the *Every Child Matters* outcomes

Earlier in this book we looked briefly at the *Every Child Matters* outcomes. In this chapter we will look in depth at how childminders can help the children in their setting to achieve the five outcomes:

- Be healthy
- Stay safe
- Enjoy and achieve
- Make a positive contribution
- Achieve economic well-being.

How can childminders help children to be healthy?

The aims of this outcome are to:

- Ensure that children and young people are physically healthy
- Ensure that children and young people are mentally and emotionally healthy
- Ensure that children and young people live healthy lifestyles.

Encouraging children to lead a healthy lifestyle is very important. By instilling the importance of being healthy from a young age we can help to combat obesity and encourage children to take responsibility for their own healthy lifestyle. Learning about healthy eating and exercise early on in life should help children to make the right choices and understand why these choices are necessary for their long-term health.

Children are naturally interested in their own bodies. They are curious about how their bodies work, how the heart beats, what the lungs are for and how their muscles work. By encouraging children to develop this interest and curiosity it will be easier to explain to them why a healthy lifestyle, i.e. a balanced diet, fresh air and exercise, is important.

First, children need to learn about healthy eating. Most children enjoy sweets, chocolate and fizzy drinks, but we now know that these foods, though nice to eat, do not provide our bodies with any nutritional value and therefore it is important that sweets and fizzy drinks are kept to a minimum and are offered rarely, perhaps as a treat, rather than regularly or in place of meals.

Some children are 'fussy eaters' and will moan and complain if they are not given the snacks and sugary foods they desire. However it is important that childminders realize that children will only 'crave' these foods for a short time until the body has been weaned off this need for sugar.

In order to provide children with a healthy diet, childminders need to understand what constitutes 'nutritional' food and how they can go about planning and preparing a menu which will both appeal to children and provide them with the necessary nutrients their bodies need.

There are five main food groups. These are:

- Bread, cereals and potatoes
- Fruit and vegetables
- Meat, fish and pulses
- Milk and dairy products
- Products containing fat and sugar.

Bread, cereals and potatoes – This category includes bread, pasta, oats, rice, noodles and breakfast cereals. Every meal offered to children should contain at least one of the food products from this group. Wholemeal bread and brown rice are preferential to white bread and white rice as they contain more nutrients.

Fruit and vegetables – This category includes all fruit and vegetables, except potatoes which are included in the above mentioned food group. You should be aiming to provide children with at least five portions of fruit and vegetables per day. Foods from this category can be fresh, canned or frozen or served as juices. If choosing canned fruit make sure that you purchase fruit in their natural juices rather than in syrup as the syrup contains a high level of sugar. Canned vegetables should be purchased in water rather than brine which contains a high level of salt.

Meat, fish and pulses – This category contains all types of meat products such as burgers and sausages, poultry, fish and eggs. Vegetarians would include soya products and tofu in this category. Lentils and pulses are also included. You should be aiming to provide two portions of food from this category per day.

Milk and dairy products – This category includes milk, cheese and yoghurt. For a healthy balanced diet you should be aiming to offer children two or three servings from this category per day.

Products containing fat and sugar – This category includes butter, margarine, oil, biscuits, cakes, ice-cream, chips and other fried foods, sweets, jam and fizzy drinks. You should be aiming to serve only small quantities from this food group on an occasional basis.

Let us now explore the five different types of nutrients which the body requires:

- Carbohydrates
- Proteins
- Fats
- Vitamins
- Minerals.

Carbohydrates – The main function of carbohydrates is to supply the body with energy. Carbohydrates can be broken down into two forms and these are 'simple' carbohydrates which can be turned into energy quickly and are found in fizzy drinks, sugar, biscuits, cakes, etc., and 'complex' carbohydrates which take longer to be turned into energy and can be found in pasta, bread, potatoes, breakfast cereals, etc. A lack of carbohydrates in the diet would result in tiredness and difficulty concentrating.

Proteins – The muscles, hair, nails, skin and internal organs of our bodies are made of protein. For our bodies to grow properly and repair themselves when necessary we need a good source of protein in our diets. Protein can be found in meat, poultry, fish, milk and milk products, eggs, beans and nuts.

Fats – Fat provides the body with energy. It also provides the body with insulation and protects our internal organs. Fats can be found in cheese, meat, butter, lard, chocolate, nuts, oily fish, etc.

Vitamins – Our bodies cannot make vitamins and therefore it is essential that we eat food products which contain them. A varied diet will ensure that we consume the correct amount of each of the vitamins listed below:

- Vitamin A is found in liver, carrots and dark green vegetables such as cabbage. Vitamin A maintains good vision, skin and hair.

- Vitamin B is found in liver, cereals, beans and eggs and helps to break down the food we eat in order for it to provide us with energy. Vitamin B also helps the body to produce blood.

- Vitamin C is found in most fresh fruit and vegetables and in particular citrus fruits such as oranges and lemons. Vitamin C helps the body to fight infection and maintain healthy skin.

- Vitamin D is found in oily fish and eggs, and helps to build strong teeth and bones.

- Vitamin E is found in whole grains, nuts and dark-green leafy vegetables such as cabbage. Vitamin E helps to protect our body cells from damage.

Minerals – Although our bodies need a huge range of minerals in order to remain healthy, the three main minerals required are iron, calcium and iodine.

In addition to the above food groups we have just looked at our bodies also need fibre and water. Fibre and water are essential for our bodies to be able to grow and function correctly, and these products are known as non-nutrient foods because they do not provide us with any energy.

In order for childminders to provide children with a healthy balanced diet they also need to take into account the child's preferences, eating habits at home, allergies and culture.

Preferences

As a childminder you should be aiming to provide the children in your care with a healthy balanced diet. However there is little point in preparing a healthy meal if you have used ingredients which the child does not like. The child's likes and dislikes should be taken into consideration when planning your menu.

Eating habits at home

This can be very difficult. If a child is used to eating 'chips with everything' at home it may be difficult to get them to enjoy a healthy meal within the childminding setting. You need to plan and prepare your meals with the parents of the children you are caring for and any issues and eating habits should come to light when discussing your meals with them. Try to work out a suitable strategy which will encourage the children and parents to adopt a healthy attitude to food both in the setting and at home.

Always start by making small, manageable changes. For example a child who has come to expect chips with every meal will find it completely unacceptable if you impose a total ban on chips. However, by reducing the amount of meals which include chips and substituting them with a healthy alternative, perhaps two or three times per week, will set the wheels in motion for a healthier lifestyle which you can then build upon in time.

Allergies

Childhood allergies can be quite common and childminders need to be prepared to work with the parents and the children they are caring for to ensure that they do not offer any food products which may be harmful to the child. Diabetes, milk allergies, coeliac disease, etc., are all complaints which may affect children.

Food intolerances and allergies occur when an individual has an unpleasant reaction to a specific food. Reactions may include:

- Vomiting

- Diarrhoea

- Abdominal pain

- Constipation

- Bloated stomach

- Skin rashes

- Headaches.

Some of the foods which are most commonly associated with intolerance and allergies are:

- Cow's milk

- Shellfish

- Nuts

- Gluten.

Diet and exercise

Although, as we have already said, ensuring that children eat a healthy diet is a major part of a childminder's job it is important, whilst instilling the need for healthy eating, that we do not become 'obsessed' with food and allow this obsession to rub off on the children, as this may lead to problems in later life such as eating disorders like anorexia and bulimia. It is not necessary to ban all foods which are not considered healthy, it is simply a case of eating these food products in moderation and not substituting chocolate bars and puddings for a healthy balanced meal. The aim of childminders is to try to get the children to understand what constitutes healthy food so that, in time, they will learn to choose these healthy options for themselves as a way of life rather than because they feel they have to!

One of the easiest ways to start children on a healthy diet is to change the way you offer snacks. Many children would opt for a biscuit and fizzy drink, however by offering a plate of brightly coloured fruits which look appealing, and freshly prepared fruit juices along with carrot sticks and raisins you will be giving the children plenty of choice from a range of healthy foods without curbing the appetite. We all eat unhealthy foods some of the time and you should not make children feel guilty for giving in to their cravings occasionally. It is when we choose unhealthy foods on a regular basis that we increase the risk of serious health problems which may last a lifetime.

In addition to offering children a healthy balanced diet it is also important that we include physical exercise in our daily routines. Physical exercise should not just be kept for outdoors although playing outdoors is essential and should be incorporated into your everyday routines in order for the children to get the fresh air they need to remain healthy.

Indoor physical exercise may come in the form of:

- Obstacle courses
- Dance
- Action rhymes
- Playing games such as 'Simon Says' and 'Musical Chairs'
- Visiting a soft play gym.

Outdoor physical exercise may come in the form of:

- Using ride-on toys
- Obstacle courses
- Ball games

- Skipping

- Races

- Visiting the park or playground.

In order for childminders to help children to be healthy they need to consider the extent to which their setting helps children to understand and adopt healthy habits, and the extent to which children can make healthy choices about what they eat and drink. For example childminders need to ensure that they:

- Offer a choice of healthy meals and snacks

- Offer healthy drinks

- Talk to the children about the importance of making healthy choices

- Discuss with the children the importance of regular exercise

- Set a good example themselves for healthy living.

In addition to exploring how to keep our bodies healthy it is also important for childminders to promote good mental health. Children need to be encouraged to sustain healthy emotional attachments with people in safe, secure and trusting relationships. We know that children thrive when their emotional needs are met, and childminders need to ensure that they nurture a child's emotional, mental, social and spiritual well-being.

Childminders can ensure that the children in their care are healthy by:

- Promoting healthy lifestyles within the setting

- Providing children with a healthy balanced diet

- Providing children with adequate exercise and outdoor activities

- Promoting physical and mental well-being

- Working in partnership with parents to ensure children are adequately supported with regard to adopting a healthy lifestyle

- Ensuring that the health needs of children and young people with learning difficulties or disabilities are addressed.

How can childminders help children to stay safe?

The aims of this outcome are to:

- Ensure that children and young people are safe from maltreatment, neglect, violence and sexual exploitation.

- Ensure that children and young people are safe from accidental injury and death.

- Ensure that children and young people are safe from bullying and discrimination

- Ensure that children have stability and are suitably cared for.

Helping children to stay safe is another essential part of a childminder's job. Adequate supervision for young children is paramount, while older children need to learn what constitutes danger and how to avoid unnecessary risks.

In addition to ensuring that children are safe indoors and that the toys and equipment you provide are clean and suitable for the ages and stages of development of the children in your care you will also need to think about issues such as:

- Safety in the garden

- Safety during planned outings
- Safety travelling to and from school
- Safety when collecting from school
- Safety when parents are dropping off and collecting children from the setting
- Safety online
- Bullying
- Stranger danger
- Abuse.

All these areas need to be carefully considered and issues arising from them need to be addressed in order for childminders to ensure that children are kept safe at all times.

Children need to be aware of how they can contribute to their own safety without being unduly frightened. Childminders can ensure the safety of the children in their care in a number of ways such as:

- By being vigilant at all times.
- Ensuring that the childminding premises both inside and out are free from potential risks.
- Ensuring that all toys and equipment are kept in a clean and good state of repair.
- Carrying out regular risk assessments.
- Actively observing the children in their care.
- Actively listening to the children in their care and responding appropriately, i.e. sharing any concerns they may have with the appropriate people.

- Teaching children how to keep themselves safe by teaching them the importance of sticking to rules, assessing risks and making the right choices.

- Keeping abreast of any training opportunities suitable for the role of childminder.

Young children are very vulnerable and it is important that they are taught how to learn about the world around them in a safe and secure manner. Every childminding setting should have rules and boundaries in terms of behaviour in order to ensure the safety and comfort of everyone present.

Childminders need to consider carefully their procedures for emergencies and evacuation and should be aware of and stick to the appropriate adult:child ratios at all times.

Childminders can ensure that the children in their care stay safe by:

- Ensuring that children and young people are aware of the potential risks to their safety and are taught how to deal with them.

- Ensuring that the childminding premises are safe and secure and free from potential danger.

- Ensuring that you are confident in dealing with issues of child protection.

- Ensuring that the safety needs of children with learning difficulties or disabilities are suitably addressed.

How can childminders help children to enjoy and achieve?

The aims of this outcome are to:

- Ensure that children are ready for starting school
- Ensure that children enjoy school
- Ensure that children and young people achieve personal and social development and enjoy recreation.

Childminders need to encourage children to develop the skills they will need for adulthood. They need to understand how to get along with others in order to get the most out of the life experiences on offer. Children need to develop confidence when playing and learning and childminders need to nurture this aspect of a child's development in order for them to enjoy the activities on offer and achieve their full potential.

In order to help a child to achieve their full potential, childminders need to look at what the child is good at and build on their interests in order to engage them enthusiastically in activities which will help to promote their all-round development.

Childminders can ensure that the children in their care enjoy and achieve by:

- Ensuring that the provision is of an excellent standard.
- Ensuring that children and young people are supported in their learning and play experiences.
- Ensuring that the provision promotes children's development and well-being and encourages them to meet early learning goals.

How can childminders help children to make a positive contribution?

The aims of this outcome are to:

- Ensure that children and young people engage in decision making and support the community and environment.

- Ensure that children and young people are aware of how to behave in a positive manner both in and out of school.

- Ensure that children and young people develop positive relationships and understand that bullying and discrimination are unacceptable.

- Ensure that children and young people develop self-confidence and are encouraged to successfully deal with significant life changes and challenges.

For children to be able to make a positive contribution they need to develop a sense of belonging. This is possible if the childminder promotes and encourages self-respect and respect of others whereby the child learns to appreciate the similarities and differences in others, and respects these similarities and differences.

Childminders need to work with the parents of the children they care for in order to meet each of the children's individual needs and a satisfactory framework for managing children's behaviour needs to be developed.

Childminders can encourage the children in their care to understand the world we live in better by providing appropriate activities and resources to enable them to explore.

Childminders can ensure the children in their care make a positive contribution by:

- Supporting their development socially and emotionally

- Supporting them through significant life changes and encouraging them to make the right decisions

- Providing them with a framework for positive behaviour.

How can childminders help children to achieve economic well-being?

The aims of this outcome are to:

- Ensure that all children and young people have access to learning resources.

- Ensure that families are supported regardless of their economic background.

Economic well-being means ensuring that no child is prevented from achieving their full potential due to economic disadvantage. Childminders need to be aware of the factors which may influence a child's achievements and be sensitive to these factors.

Childminders need to provide a welcoming environment and make sure that they are approachable in order to break down any barriers which may exist and enable the child to feel they belong in the setting.

All children learn in a warm and welcoming environment with knowledgeable adults they can trust and relate to, and it is important that childminders show an interest in the child and build on the relationship they have with them and their family.

Childminders can ensure the children in their care achieve economic well-being by:

- Ensuring that children and young people are treated as individuals, regardless of their family background
- Listening to and respecting parents
- Ensuring that children are treated fairly
- Ensuring that children are included.

Exercise: Think of at least one way in which you can help children in your setting to:

- Be healthy
- Stay safe
- Enjoy and achieve
- Make a positive contribution
- Achieve economic well-being.

Chapter Six
Planning for children

The importance of planning

Planning is an integral part of a successful childminding business. Although there is no right or wrong way to plan, the method you choose must be easy for you to implement and will need to take into account the specific individual needs of each child in your care.

If you sit and think about the number of plans you make on a daily basis you would probably be amazed at your findings. Everyone makes plans every day. These plans are unlikely to be written down but our everyday lives are based on short- and long-term plans. Important events such as a wedding or birthday party are often planned well in advance with lists of things to do, guests to invite and outfits to wear. Everyday routines such as shopping trips and cooking meals are also planned. Before we can begin to bake a cake, for example, we need to check that we have the right ingredients and make a list of what we need to buy. Of course, not all of the plans we make every day are methodical in this way. You may start your day mentally planning what you are about to do. Get up, have a shower, get dressed, eat breakfast, wash up, make the bed, etc. A large part of a childminder's day may be taken up with school, nursery and playgroup runs, nappy changing and feeding. However, the times in between need to be planned carefully in order to enable the childminder to put some structure into their day and for the children to benefit from suitable activities and experiences, rather than to spend the day being ferried about, fed and changed with little or no quality time for playing and learning.

Childminders need to know how to plan their day so that the activities and experiences they offer the children enable them to experience variation, in order for them to benefit from their time in the setting. Planning our day enables us to look carefully at the activities on offer and to ensure that there is sufficient time to carry out the intended activities in order for the children to gain something from the experience. For example, there is little point in deciding to have a baking session with the children at 3.00 p.m. if you have to leave to collect children from school at 3.20 p.m. The activity will either be rushed or abandoned, both of which will be of no benefit to the children. In order for this activity to be a success and for the children to enjoy and learn from it the childminder needs to plan sufficient time to bake including considering how long it will take to weigh and mix the ingredients, how long the ingredients will take to cook and how long it will take to clear away and wash up, as these are all necessary aspects of the task.

Although planning is vital when considering children's individual needs it is also important to understand the whole of the planning cycle including being able to implement the plans and decide whether they are suitable for the children. Childminders need to:

Plan – Think carefully about the children in your care; their ages, their abilities and their preferences. What type of activities do you consider to be beneficial for them? There is little point in preparing to bake a cake if the children you are caring for are too young to help. Likewise providing baby toys and rattles for a 3 year old will not be beneficial.

Implement – Think carefully about the activities you have planned and decide on the best time for the children to take part in each. Make sure there is sufficient time for the children to actively take part without rushing them. Try to avoid planning complex activities at a time of the day when the children are likely to be too tired to enjoy them.

Observe and assess – There is little point in planning and implementing any activity if you are unfamiliar with how to observe and assess the children to ensure that the activities are suitable. Is the activity too hard or too easy? Do the children appear to be enjoying what they are doing? Are they actively involved? Are they bored?

Evaluate – Finally, after observing and assessing the children whilst they are taking part in the activity you have planned, you should be able to decide whether the activity has been a success or not. Can the activity be expanded upon? Would you consider repeating the activity? If not, why not? Can the activity be improved?

It is important to remember that not all planning results in endless paperwork. Planning can be just as effective if it is done informally and, experienced childminders are usually planning instinctively with great success. One of the responsibilities of a childminder is to provide the children in their care with the best start to their early education and this can be done with careful thought about the activities they provide which will give them a head start in learning whilst having fun and will follow through to their formal school years. One of the main reasons parents choose a childminder to care for their child, over a nursery, is that they can offer everyday learning experiences in the home setting which educate children while they are having fun. Simple tasks such as setting the table and sorting the laundry can be useful to promote early numeracy; pairing socks, sorting colours, counting how many knives, forks and spoons are needed, etc. Not only do these tasks encourage a child's early education they do so while helping them to develop in every way rather than in the formal setting of a nursery or classroom.

Although not all planning needs to be written down, it is an essential part of a childminder's work to be able to provide evidence of their planning during their Ofsted inspection, therefore it is necessary to get into the practice of writing down your plans. By building up a collection of planned activities and recording and evaluating them, you will be able to refer to them in the future.

Planning is very personal. No two childminders will plan their play and learning opportunities in the same way, quite simply because we are all unique and we will be caring for children who are also unique. The abilities and needs of each child may differ enormously and effective planning will take into account each child's personal requirements. There is no right or wrong way to plan your activities providing the method you choose is effective.

Writing and implementing curriculum plans

It is important for practitioners to understand the difference in short-, medium- and long-term plans in order to understand how to plan their work. Initially you will need to work out, with the child's parents, exactly what you are hoping to achieve with the planned activity. For example, you could be trying to teach a child how to recognize the four primary colours. Your final goal will be to get the child to recognize these colours, however, before reaching this 'long-term' goal you will have set the child a 'short-term' and 'medium-term' goal which, once achieved, will result in them reaching the long-term goal of recognizing the primary colours. You will need to decide on a time frame for achieving each of the goals, the length of which will be dependent on the complexity of what you are hoping the child will learn. A short-term plan may cover a week, medium term a month and finally, after six months the child may have achieved the long-term goal.

Some childminders find it easier to plan their activities around a theme or topic and these can be tailored to suit the likes and preferences of the children in your care. Themes and topics can be planned according to the time of the year for example, spring, summer, autumn or winter and the children can be encouraged to take part in activities associated with these seasons. You may like to do a display for the wall or take the children on a nature walk looking for colourful leaves in the autumn or pretty flowers in the summer. Celebrations such as Christmas, Easter, Divali and the Chinese New Year also provide excellent themes for planning children's learning and play.

Depending on the age of the children you are caring for you may also like to introduce topics such as colours, numbers, shapes and telling the time into your everyday planning. It is always important to remember that, although useful, plans should not restrict children from being allowed to play spontaneously, and time should always be allowed for free play with planned activities interspersed.

The Early Years Foundation Stage makes it clear to practitioners that planning for the children in their care should begin with what is already known about the children you have in your setting. It stands to reason therefore that all planning should be based on the stage the children are already at and build on from this stage. Childminders need to:

- Collect evidence about the children in their care – this can be done through observations and by talking with the child's parents, teachers or previous practitioners.

- Assess the evidence they have – you need to look at the evidence you have collected about the child and use this to decide what action you need to take.

- Use the evidence to plan suitable activities and experiences – with the evidence you have collected you need to plan suitable experiences for play both inside and outside allowing for the child to initiate these experiences whenever possible.

- Effectively implement their plans – you need to use the environment and resources to implement the plans you have made, supporting the children where necessary.

- Evaluate their practice – you need to critically examine your practice to evaluate whether you have met the needs of all of the children in your setting and decide how you can effectively extend the children's learning experiences.

As I have previously mentioned, planning for children's learning and development can be divided into three categories, namely short, medium and long term.

Short-term planning

Short-term planning is concerned with differentiation and planning for the needs of specific groups and individual children. This type of planning provides the detail of activities, experiences, resources, etc., that the childminder has identified through ongoing observations and assessments of the children in their care. Short-term planning can be used for a specific activity or perhaps for a full day or week's activities.

Medium-term planning

Medium-term planning allows us to look at the continuity and progression of children from one stage in each area of their learning to the next. This type of planning allows us to identify the concepts, knowledge, attitudes and skills of the children over a specified period of time.

Long-term planning

This type of planning is concerned with the child's entitlement to a broad and balanced curriculum. The Areas of Learning and Development in the EYFS are achieved through long-term planning over an appropriate length of time. Therefore a childminder, with the aim of helping a child to recognize the four primary colours, may create a curriculum plan like the example given in the figure below.

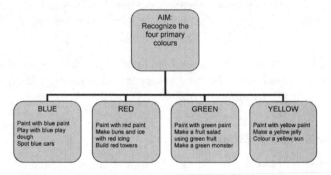

Fig 6.1 *Primary colours*

When writing curriculum plans for children it is very important that we ask ourselves some questions in order to be sure that the plans we intend to implement are both effective and useful.

Before deciding which activities to focus on, ask yourself:

- What activities/experiences/resources will meet the learning outcomes I have in mind for the children?

- Do the activities/experiences/resources support the learning of *all* the children in my care?

- Are the activities/experiences/resources inclusive?

- What am I intending to teach the children?

- Why have I chosen this particular activity/experience/resource?

You then need to think about how you will assess the children while they are taking part in the activity/experience you have planned:

- Will I assess the children during or after the activity?
- What method of assessment is most suitable?
- Do I need to save samples of work?
- Do I need to take photographs?

Finally you will need to evaluate the activity by asking yourself:

- Was the activity/experience a success?
- Were the intended learning outcomes achieved?
- If not, why not?
- What did the children learn?
- What did I learn?
- How can I improve things?
- Do I need to re-evaluate my short/medium-term plans?
- What other activities/experiences/resources can I provide to encourage the children to achieve the intended learning outcomes?

Exercise: Write a curriculum plan which will encourage children to recognize the numbers 1–10.

One of the most important, and often difficult, aspects of a childminder's job is being able to successfully plan and provide care and suitable activities and learning experiences for children of mixed-age groups. Many childminders will care for children of school age in addition to babies and pre-school children. Although it is true to say that, on most days, the school-age children will be spending the majority of their day away from the childminding setting while they are in school, it is important to think carefully about how you will provide adequate stimulation and resources for these children both before and after school and during school holidays. Older children should not be expected to take second place and to have their play restricted because of the younger ones, although there may be times when older children will need to consider the ages of the younger ones when requesting certain activities.

Childminders need to carefully consider the toys, books and other resources they provide and make sure that these are suitable for *all* the ages and stages of development of the children they are caring for. For example 8 year olds should not be expected to play with baby and toddler toys, and teenagers should not have to make do with immature reading material.

All children learn through play and first-hand experiences and it is the duty of the childminder to provide each child with sufficient resources which are appropriate to their age and stage of development in order to provide entertaining and stimulating experiences. Although the way in which the childminder plans their day and the activities they provide influences the way in which the children play and learn, other factors also have an affect such as the number and ages of the other children in the setting and the amount of quality time the childminder actually spends interacting with the children are very important factors.

All children need their play and learning activities to be planned and structured. This includes young babies and toddlers as well as older children. The activities, resources and experiences you provide must be appropriate to the age and stage of development of each individual child in your care and children should not be expected to 'make do' with what you have if these items are clearly unsuitable.

Observing, assessing and evaluating children

Before we can fully understand how to carry out an observation or an assessment we must first understand what each definition really means.

Observation

Observation involves the gathering of information about a particular child's behaviour and their stage of development. It will be necessary for you to seek parental approval before carrying out an observation of a child. When seeking parental approval you will need to inform the parents of the following:

1. Why you feel an observation would be beneficial.

2. What you are hoping your observation will achieve or reveal.

3. How you feel the observation will assist you in planning for the child's future needs.

You will also need to reassure the parents that you will share the information from the observation with them and that all the details will remain confidential and will be accessed only by them, yourself and any other professionals on a 'need to know basis'. Always point out to the parents that the reason for an observation is to focus on the *positive* aspects of the child's behaviour and progress rather than looking to produce a *negative* list of underachievement.

Observing a child means that you are watching and studying what they do. You will be observing children all the time while they are in your care to make sure they are safe, to make sure they have the appropriate toys and equipment to play with, to see whether they are tired or hungry or whether they need a nappy change. This kind or observation will come automatically to you as you are a professional person who is knowledgeable about the care of young children and you are aware of their needs and requirements. There are however many more reasons why it is necessary for you to observe children, such as:

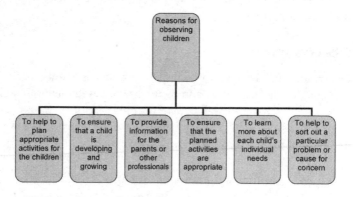

Fig 6.2 *Reasons for observing children*

The nature of a childminder's job means that you will be very busy throughout your working day and it is therefore necessary for you to choose a method of observing and assessing the children in your care which is easy for you to understand and, more importantly, implement. Try not to see observation and assessment as an additional task but as an essential one which will enable you to be aware of the things the children in your care can do, what they are almost capable of doing and what they need assistance with. Observing and assessing children will not only help you to pinpoint where a child is at in terms of development and growth, but it will also help you to identify any problems or concerns.

There are several methods of observing children and each individual will have their own preference as to which method they prefer. It may be necessary for you to use several methods of observation during the course of your work depending on whether you require a quick, informal observation or an in-depth account. The figure below shows some of the different ways of observing children.

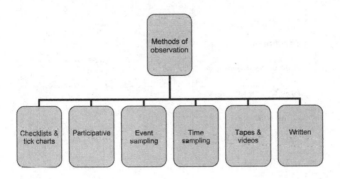

Fig 6.3 *Methods of observation*

Checklists and tick charts – This can be particularly useful to record what stage a child is at for example, how many colours they can recognize, how many numbers they can count in sequence, whether or not they can recognize the letters of the alphabet. Checklists and tick charts are quick and simple to use and are particularly helpful at future dates to see how a child has developed and whether there are any changes since the last observation.

A tick chart may look something like this:

TICK CHART

Name of child

Age of child

Date

Activity	X	✓
Able to hold a paintbrush		
Able to hold a pencil		
Able to use scissors to cut paper		
Able to tie a shoe lace		
Able to fasten a button		
Able to catch a ball		
Able to throw a ball		
Able to kick a ball		
Able to ride a bicycle		

Fig 6.4   *Tick chart*

Obviously the statements you insert in your own tick chart will depend on the age of the child you are observing. For example if you are using this method to observe a 9-month-old baby the statements may read something like:

- Able to sit up unaided
- Able to pull themselves to a standing position

- Able to roll from front to back

- Able to roll from back to front

- Able to clap hands

- Able to wave goodbye

- Able to crawl, etc.

Participative observations – These are when you yourself actually take part in the activity with the child. The main disadvantage of this type of observation is that it can be difficult for you to write notes and record what is happening at the actual time, and you may therefore have to rely heavily on your memory to record your observations at a later date.

Event sampling – See next page, fig. 6.5. This is often used to record patterns of behaviour. Generally speaking, event sampling is useful to record an area of a child's behaviour which you and the child's parents would ideally like to change for example temper tantrums. By recording exactly what happens prior to the child's tantrum it is possible to spot 'triggers' in behaviour which, if managed correctly, can be eliminated.

Time sampling – This is another form of event sampling, only this time you observe what the child is doing at fixed intervals throughout the day for example, every hour throughout the whole day or every 30 minutes throughout the afternoon.

Tapes and videos – These are really only beneficial for observing children if they are not aware of their presence. You may find that a child who knows that a video camera is pointing at them will play up and act out of character, making your observation unnatural and therefore ineffective. A tape recorder may be easier to hide but the disadvantage here would be background noise if you are caring for several children. If you do choose to use tapes and videos to observe the children in your care, make sure that

Name: Sam

Age: 3 years 4 months

Aim: To ascertain what triggers Sam's temper tantrums

Date: 13 April 2008

Times observations took place: 11.35 a.m. – 12.30 p.m.

4.15 p.m. – 5.00 p.m.

EVENT	TIME	WHAT HAPPENED?	COMMENTS
1	11.35 a.m.	Sam approached a child who was happily playing with the cars and took the toys from him.	Sam had a tantrum – he seems to have difficulty acknowledging that he cannot have toys on demand when someone else is playing with them.
2	12.10 p.m.	Sam refused to sit at the table for lunch because he wanted to sit where someone else was already sat.	Sam threw a tantrum.
3	4.35 p.m.	The parent of another child came to collect – Sam wanted his mum to collect him.	Sam threw a tantrum because someone else was going home before him.

Fig 6.5 *Event sampling*

you always get the written permission of the parents before making any form of recording of their child.

Written observations – These help us to record information about a child's growth and development or their behaviour over a short period of time. Written observations require very little planning and preparation and can usually be done quickly at any time.

It is important, when observing children, that the information you gather is accurate, however, you must also be aware of your own limits and not attempt to put your own diagnosis to a problem or concern. While the information you have gathered and recorded may well be useful it is the responsibility of other professionals to diagnose a child.

Now that we have looked at *methods* of observations, let us take a look at the *types* of observation. The main types of observation are as follows:

- Naturalistic
- Structured
- Longitudinal
- Snapshot.

Naturalistic – These are so-called because they are observations of children which are carried out in the child's usual surroundings. The observation allows the child to carry out tasks which they would normally carry out without any structuring being attempted by you, the observer.

Structured – This type of observation is the opposite of naturalistic in that the childminder has specifically set up a particular activity in order to observe how a child carries out a specific task. For example an obstacle course could be created to observe a child's balance and coordination, or a painting activity to observe a child's fine motor skills.

Longitudinal – When you have settled into a pattern of regularly observing the children in your care and recording your findings you will build up your own longitudinal records of observation as your findings will show how the children in your care change and progress over a lengthy period of time. Each child's set of records and observations will be their *longitudinal* record which will enable the important adults in their lives namely you, their childminder, and their parents to identify the important milestones and achievements in their lives.

Snapshot – As the name suggests this type of observation involves trying to achieve a 'snapshot' of how a child is behaving at any given period of time. For example a snapshot observation of how a child reacts immediately after their parent has dropped them off may be helpful in trying to deal with a child who is clingy and difficult to settle.

With all observations there is a certain amount of essential information which must be included, such as:

- The name of the child

- The age of the child

- The date the observation was carried out

- The activity the child was involved in during the time the observation took place

- The number, ages and gender of any other children involved in the activity

- The name of the person carrying out the observation.

When carrying out an observation of a child, using whichever method you are most comfortable with and which is appropriate for the purpose it is intended, it is vital that you remember that the observation must be accurate and unbiased. Refrain from adding or taking away findings which you feel may upset or worry parents, as these may be vital clues to the overall assessment of the child. For example, if you are observing a child's behaviour in order to develop an appropriate strategy to deal with tantrums, and you omit the fact that, during an observation, the child lashed out or threw a toy across the room, simply to avoid embarrassing the child's parents, then you risk jeopardizing the whole exercise as this is an important part of the child's behaviour which needs to be addressed. Never exaggerate the situation or problem to make it appear worse than it really is. Your observations must be accurate and up to date to have any benefit whatsoever to the child's overall development.

The observations you have carried out will stand you in good stead when deciding on how to plan for the needs of the children in your care. For example your observations and assessments will enable you to:

- See which activities a child enjoys the most

- See which activities a child is least interested in

- Determine which activities a child is good at

- Decide how to extend the activity in order to stretch the skills of the child

- Check the child's progress and growth.

The more information you have about a child in your care, the better equipped you should be to provide for their needs. Always take your cue from the child and never try to overstretch them before they are ready. When you have found an activity which the child enjoys, introduce it as often as they wish but refrain from extending it until they are competent enough to cope with more complexity. If you try to push a child too far too soon you risk alienating them and their self-confidence may even suffer as a result if they feel they have failed in a particular task.

A 2-year-old child who has just discovered the joy of painting for example by using a variety of finger-paints, paint pads and sponges should be allowed to experiment before you introduce more complex materials such as brushes, scrapers, stamps, string, etc. Avoid the temptation to indulge them with too many varied and complex materials before they are ready and always be realistic with your expectations.

Likewise there is little point in planning an activity involving making a collage with a child who cannot yet use scissors correctly. Instead allow the child the time to practise using scissors on a regular basis and then, when they are confident with this task, introduce making a simple collage.

Assessment

Assessment is your own unbiased, objective reflection on the information you have gathered during your observation. Before finalizing your assessment, you should discuss your observational findings with the child's parents and, if necessary any other professionals, in order for them to add their own comments, opinions and ideas. The results of your assessment should form an essential part of your future planning and they should be used to monitor the child's progress.

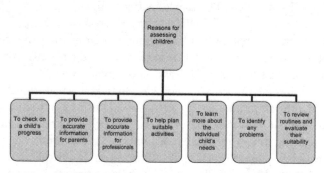

Fig 6.6   *Reasons for assessing children*

There is little point in carrying out observations on the children in your care if, after doing these observations, you do not assess your findings. As a childminder you will have the advantage of knowing the children in your care well and be in a position to work with them closely on a daily basis. This closeness will enable you to see how the children are growing and developing. By using your observations you will be able to assess the point each child is at and you will then be able to plan appropriate routines and activities to suit each individual child. You need to be aware of the importance of routines being changed as the children you are caring for grow and develop, and your observations will enable you to see easily when a child is ready to move on to a more complex activity.

Planning, observing and assessing children are all very important aspects of a childminder's duties, however without evaluation all of the other tasks will have been a waste of time.

Evaluation

This is the method of judging how much progress the child has actually made over a period of time. Evaluations need to be continuous and systematic and they need to take into account the child's past experiences.

Children are changing all the time and this is why evaluations need to be carried out. As the children grow and progress, you will need to alter your routines and activities to take into account these changes. Childminders will benefit from evaluating not only the children in their care and the activities they provide, but also the materials and resources they have on offer and the space and time available.

Evaluations will enable you to:

- Help the children to progress in certain areas of their development.

- Encourage the children to develop an interest in a variety of areas and activities.

- Ascertain whether the children are playing well together and if there are any areas of behaviour which are causing concern.

- Decide whether the toys and equipment available are appropriate for the ages and stages of development the children are currently at, and which new toys and equipment may be of benefit.

- Decide whether any new learning materials will benefit the children.

- Ascertain whether the activities already enjoyed are stretching the ability and imagination of the children appropriately, and whether these need to be assessed.

By observing, assessing and evaluating the children in your care you will be able to build up an accurate picture of each child, based on their individuality and preference. Any preconceived ideas of what you personally *expect* from each child must be forgotten and you should aim at all times to avoid speculation or allowing yourself to be influenced by prior knowledge. Avoid making comparisons and remember that all children are individuals, unique in every aspect of their makeup and should be treated with understanding, love and respect.

When evaluating your observations and assessments there may be times when it is apparent to you that something is amiss and that a certain course of action may be necessary. For example, your observations may have revealed a medical problem which may need referral. Always discuss your findings and worries with the child's parents and decide, together, what course of action should be taken. Be sensitive to the feelings of the parents if you suspect their child has some kind of medical problem and take the time to offer support and reassurance. Often something like a hearing impairment is short-lived and may be the result of a particularly heavy cold; however more severe problems will need ongoing treatment and parents may feel very vulnerable at this time.

Chapter Seven
Essential paperwork

Contracts and how to complete them

It is absolutely essential that you have a watertight contract to use
in your childminding setting. The contract must be clear and
legible with no room for ambiguity. The contract must cover all
the main, relevant points and must be signed by all parties
concerned.

If you decide to draft your own contracts then it is paramount that
you think carefully about what you need to include so that you do
not leave anything open to chance thereby avoiding disagreements
at a later date.

There are the obvious points which most people will remember to
include such as the days and hours required and the fees payable,
but it is also essential that the less obvious things are not
overlooked such as who will be responsible for payment, what
does the fee include, who will collect the child, how much will be
charged for late payments or late collections? At the start of a
placement it is easy to be trusting and, in an ideal world, everyone
would stick to their side of the bargain, however, in reality, this is
rarely the case and, should parents start to take advantage of your
good nature it is always easier to rectify problems by referring to
the contract as backup *providing* you have included all the relevant
points.

Begin your childminding relationships with prospective parents in a professional manner. It is likely that you will know very little about the families you work with initially and often discussing topics like fees can be uncomfortable, however, it is important that you overcome these feelings from the start and that you are decisive and confident when negotiating a contract in order to avoid problems at a later date. A written contract is a condition of a childminder's registration in England and Wales and you should ensure that *all* relevant information is included if you are to protect yourself. Verbal agreements, even with the very best of intentions, will come unstuck at some point.

Most childminders will probably use either specially prepared contracts which can be purchased through organizations such as the National Childminding Association or they will produce their own written or computer generated contracts. It is perfectly acceptable to compose your own contracts providing you are confident about producing such a document and are careful to include all the important points.

Contracts are necessary for several reasons including:

- They set out formally what you, the childminder, is willing to do and what you expect from the parents/carers without any misunderstandings.

- Contracts show that you are a professional person working in a businesslike fashion.

- Contracts can be personalized to take into account the differing needs for childcare, for example a young baby requiring full day care or a 7 year old requiring before- and after-school care.

It is important, when completing contracts, that you take the time to sit down with the child's parents or carers and go through each section of the contract with them so that they completely understand what they are agreeing to. Any concerns should be discussed *prior* to anyone signing the contract and these should be cleared up to the satisfaction of everyone involved.

It is important when completing contracts that you do not agree to something which may later have an adverse effect on either the way you carry out your business or the other children in your setting. Be firm and do not allow yourself to be pressurized into agreeing to something which is not practical. Remember the contract is a *mutual* agreement stating what both parties are happy to do.

When you and the parents are both happy with the content of the contract, sign and date it. You should keep one copy and the parents or carers should retain the other copy. In the case of involvement of any agencies such as Social Services they would also retain a copy of the contract.

Contracts should be reviewed regularly. It is always a good idea to incorporate a review date on the contract to go through the routine arrangements and to ensure that everyone is still happy with the arrangement. This could be every six or 12 months, however it is also important that the contract is reviewed immediately any changes are made. For example, if the parent increases their working hours or changes the days they require childcare then this must be recorded and the contract updated accordingly.

If you decide to create your own contract it is important that you take the time to think carefully about all the aspects you will need to include such as:

- Your full details including your name, address, telephone number, registration number, insurance details, etc.

- The child's full name, address and date of birth

- The parents' or carer's full names, addresses and contact details

- Contracted days and hours

- The fees payable including whether these fees are payable in advance or in arrears, whether they are payable weekly, monthly or termly, whether they include bank holidays, retainers or a deposit

- Details of holidays and any payments due during these periods

- Details of sickness and payments due during these periods

- Details of any unsociable or overnight care

- Details of any charges made for late payment, early drop offs or late collections

- Details of who is responsible for paying the fees

- Details of who is responsible for paying any additional fees such as pre-school, school clubs or routine outings

- Details of what is included in the fee, for example meals and snacks, nappies, formula milk, toiletries, etc.

- Notice of termination required on both sides

- Review date of the contract

- Details of any special arrangements

- Details of any settling in periods

- Details of what the parent will be expected to provide for their child i.e. waterproofs in winter if you have to walk the children to school, a comforter or dummy if the child requires these, nappies, formula milk, etc.

There are one or two other things which you may need to consider, although these are more personal and will only be relevant to some of the families you work with.

Caring for children from the same family – Are you prepared to offer concessions for siblings? You should think carefully before offering concessions and only do so if you can afford the loss in earnings. Make it clear on your contract that the concession is given to the *oldest* child and that when they leave the setting your regular fee will apply to the remaining child.

Maternity leave – If a parent already using your service is expecting a baby, she may wish to keep her older child with her during her maternity period while requesting that you keep a place open for both this child and the new baby. Under these circumstances you would be well advised to terminate the original contract and draw up a new one to cover the period of maternity leave. You may wish to negotiate part-time paid hours for the older child and/or a retainer fee to hold the place. A retainer fee cannot however be charged for the baby until after it is born. A new contract should then be negotiated once the mother has returned to work and both her children are in your setting.

School holidays – You may be asked to care for the child of a schoolteacher. If the parent decides that they wish to keep their child with them during school holidays then you should negotiate a retainer fee. Think carefully about the drop-in earnings and make sure that this is a feasible option for you before agreeing to it.

Record forms and how to complete them

In addition to having a contract it is essential that childminders draw up an accurate record of all the children in their care. This record should contain details such as:

- The child's full name, address and date of birth.

- The address and contact details of the child's parents including work details.

- Details of who is authorized to drop the child off and collect them from the childminding setting.

- Details of the 'password' if this is necessary. Sometimes parents may need to arrange for someone else to collect their child. Ideally you will have already met this person however, in unavoidable situations this may not be the case. If the child is too young to recognize the person collecting them then it is a good idea to have a password known only to you, the child's parents and of course the person collecting. If the person collecting does not know the password *do not* hand the child over to them. Even with a password in place, if you are in any doubt whatsoever about the validity of a person calling to collect a child, do not hand them over. Telephone the parent for confirmation first.

- Details of the child's general practitioner.

- Details of any health problems or ongoing medical treatment such as inhalers for asthma.

- Details of any immunizations the child has had.

- Details of the child's likes and dislikes.

- Details of the child's first language and any other languages they may speak away from the childminding setting.

Medical forms and how to complete them

Before you can give a child any form of medication, injection or carry out any invasive procedure you must have the written permission of the child's parents and have undergone any necessary training that enables you to carry out these procedures competently.

Upon signed permission from the parents you will also need to know:

- What the medicine is for and how it should affect the child so that you will know if it is working.

- The exact time the medicine needs to be taken and whether it is necessary to administer before or after meals.

- The exact dose required.

- When the medication was last given.

- The necessary procedure to follow if the medication does not appear to be working.

- How you should store the medicine for example does it need to go in the fridge or be kept at room temperature?

- How the medication should be given to the child, for example orally, using a spoon or syringe, or injected.

- Whether the medication produces any side effects.

- What procedure you should follow in the event that you forget to administer the medicine at the stated time.

As with contracts and record forms, specially prepared medical forms can be purchased from organizations such as the National Childminding Association.

Attendance registers

Childminders need to complete an attendance register which sets out the number of children you care for and their ages. The Ofsted inspector will request to see this register when carrying out your

Month *April 2008*

Name of Child *David*

Date of Birth of Child *02/01/2006*

Week commencing: *7 April 2008*

Day	Time of Arrival	Time of Departure	No. of Hours
Monday	*7.45 a.m.*	*5.45 p.m.*	*10*
Tuesday	*9.00 a.m.*	*4.00 p.m.*	*7*
Wednesday	*9.00 a.m.*	*4.00 p.m.*	*7*
Thursday	*9.00 a.m.*	*4.00 p.m.*	*7*
Friday			*0*
Saturday			*0*
Sunday			*0*
Total hours			*31 hours*

Childminder's signature ....

Parent's signature ....

Fig 7.1   *Child's Attendance Record*

inspection. It is important that you get into the habit of completing your register *regularly*. It is preferable to fill in your register every day when the children arrive at and leave your setting, however, at the very least you should aim to do this every week. Leaving it any longer will result in you having to rely heavily on your memory and, if you have several children coming and going, it may not be possible to remember the times each child arrived at and departed from your setting.

Attendance registers are very important and they need to be accurate and up to date. Always get the parent to sign their child's attendance record at the end of each week to prove their agreement of the hours their child was in your care. This is particularly useful in the case of an accident or illness when you may need to refer to your attendance record to clarify when the child was in your setting.

Once again, you may like to purchase a pre-printed attendance register from the National Childminding Association but it is also perfectly acceptable to produce your own. And, if you choose to do this, you may like to consider the example in fig 7.1.

Accounts

Many self-employed people shudder at the thought of being responsible for their accounts. The key to successful accounting is to do it *regularly*. Keeping up with your accounts by doing little and often is preferable to leaving them for months and then frantically having to search for vital receipts at the end of the tax year.

Like all self-employed people, childminders are responsible for keeping accurate tax and business records, regardless of whether they need to pay income tax or not. You will need to register for tax and National Insurance contributions as a self-employed person and you can do this by visiting www.hmrc.gov.uk/ startingup/register.htm, or by telephoning HM Revenue and Customs on their helpline number 0845 915 4515.

The accounts you keep must contain details of all the money you receive and spend through your work as a childminder and you must retain these records for six years and you are obliged, by law, to ensure that the records you keep support the figures you enter on your tax return.

You will need to be aware of what your costs are for running your business before you can successfully decide on how much to charge for your service. It is not a good idea to *guess* at a rate nor base your fees on the *going rate* for your area, although obviously you will need to take this into consideration in order not to set your fees too high or too low. It is worth bearing in mind the following expenditure when calculating the costs you will incur as a childminder on either a weekly or annual basis.

ANNUAL COSTS	WEEKLY COSTS
Registration fee payable to Ofsted	Food and drink purchased for the children you are childminding.
Public liability and household insurance.	Wages for yourself and any assistant you may employ, including NIC and income tax.
National Childminding Association membership fee (if applicable).	Items such as paper, paints, craft materials, etc.
Training costs for professional development including first aid training.	Travel expenses incurred while carrying our your childminding duties, such as petrol to take the children to clubs, schools, etc.
Wear and tear on premises and equipment.	The cost of activities, outings and treats for the children you are childminding.
Heat, light, water, etc. – increased household bills.	Birthday cards and gifts for the children you care for in your childminding work.
Equipment and toys.	
Christmas presents for the children you care for in your childminding work.	

Fig 7.2   *Annual and weekly costs*

It is, of course, entirely up to you how you decide to keep your accounts. There is no set way, and it is very much a matter of personal preference. However, what you must make sure is that your records are accurate and up to date. Many people choose to set up their accounts on a personal computer and there are many suitable computer software programs available. However, if you prefer to have handwritten accounts these too are perfectly acceptable and an accounts book with pre-printed columns can be bought from many high street stores. Accounts books can also be purchased from the National Childminding Association and these are straightforward and easy to understand. Your accounts should be neat and accurate so that you can see, at a glance, what you have earned, what you have spent and any profit or loss you have made.

The example shown in the figure on the next page is one way of setting out income and expenditure. The trick is to find a method that works for you and to be disciplined when completing your accounts. Set aside some time say, once a week or once a month, when you can devote yourself to getting your accounts up to date. By being organized you will save yourself a lot of hassle in the long run. Make sure you keep all your receipts and number these. You can then write the number of the receipt next to the item it relates to on your account sheet so that you can see easily which receipt matches which expense. It is a good idea to either staple the receipts to the appropriate page of your accounts or keep them in numerical order in a separate folder.

As I have mentioned before the way you set out your accounts is entirely up to you and you should look for a method of recording your earnings and expenses which works for you and which you find easy to use.

By adding up the figures in each of the columns headed 'amount' you will be able to see, at a glance, how much money you have received for the month and how much money you have spent.

INCOME			EXPENDITURE		
DATE	ITEM	AMOUNT	DATE	ITEM	AMOUNT
07/04/08	Fees – David Sam	 75.00 25.00	07/04/08	Food for children's teas	6.35
14/04/08	Fees – Cathy	 15.00	14/04/08	Paper Paint Glitter	4.99 6.50 .99
21/04/08	Fees – Cathy Sam	 15.00 25.00	21/04/08	Petrol	25.00
28/04/08	Fees – Cathy Milk refund	 15.00 13.75	28/04/08	Postage to NCMA Toilet rolls Professional carpet clean	 .28 4.99 25.00

Fig 7.3   *Income and expenditure*

If you choose to set up your own accounts system, it is important that you are accurate and that you are aware of the items which the Inland Revenue will allow you to set against your tax liability.

Diaries and what to include

Many childminders choose to furnish parents of young children with a 'diary'. Although at first this may seem like even more paperwork, diaries can prove invaluable to both parents and practitioners. Diaries can be used to record a baby or young child's basic daily routine with you and the diary goes back and forth between the child's home and the childminding setting. Both parents and childminders can also use the book to record additional information such as what the baby has been like over the weekend, any new developments, any medicinal arrangements, holiday dates, etc. Although the diary should not take the place of face-to-face conversation it can prove effective for parents who are often in a rush in the morning and worry that they may forget to tell you something important.

A typical page from a diary written for a 15-month-old child may read something like this:

Monday 14 April
Breakfast – Lucinda ate half a bowl of porridge with sliced banana and drank all her milk.
Lunch – Lucinda ate all her lunch today, she had cottage pie, carrots and cauliflower followed by yoghurt.
Tea – Lucinda ate very little at teatime. She had ¼ of a cheese sandwich, some melon slices and a fromage frais.

From this diary entry Lucinda's parents are able to see at a glance what their daughter has eaten throughout the day. If she appears hungry towards the end of the day they will be able to see that this is probably because Lucinda ate little at teatime at the childminder's.

The childminder should also record the child's nappy changes or potty/toilet routines. A child who has not had a bowel movement for a couple of days may be in some discomfort. Often this sort of thing can get overlooked as the parent may think that the child has gone to the toilet in the childminding setting, and the childminder will think that the child has had a bowel movement at home. By recording this information it is easy to see at a glance whether there is any cause for concern.

Likewise, a tired child can easily be identified if the childminder records sleep patterns, or if the parent uses the diary to inform the childminder if they have had a bad night with the child waking often.

A brief description of the child's overall day, like the example below, stating what they have enjoyed in the setting is often appreciated by parents who then feel they have had an insight into what their child is doing in their absence. Always try to involve parents as much as possible in the care of their child even if they cannot be with them.

> Lucinda has enjoyed her day in the setting. She has enjoyed finger-painting using a variety of colours and has also produced some beautiful pictures using sponges and rollers. She has also enjoyed taking part in outdoor play using the ride on toys and playing in the sand and water tray. She has managed to complete several jigsaws with some support, listened to stories and enjoyed singing songs and dressing up.

Writing policies

As a self-employed person running your own business from home it is important to always remember that, although you are providing a service, your house is still your home and as such should be treated with respect.

You will need to decide, prior to any child entering your setting, what your boundaries are going to be and how you are going to implement them. It is a good idea to think carefully about your aims and goals and write your policies to reflect these. Any policy you draw up should be displayed on the walls of your setting and a copy of each policy should be given to the parents of the child before a placement commences. Some childminders ask parents to sign a form to say that they understand and agree to their policies to avoid any future misunderstandings but this is simply a matter of preference.

There are several main areas for which you may like to implement a policy.

Behaviour – Most parents accept the need for children to have boundaries when it comes to behaviour; however it is important to realize that not all parents will share your views when it comes to discipline. You can usually determine early on whether or not a set of parents share your own views and values and this is one of the reasons why it is important to discuss things such as behaviour at the initial interview. You should be able to tell at this stage whether or not you feel able to work with the parents or whether you feel there would be too many conflicting opinions for you to offer suitable childcare. This is why I would never advise you to sign a contract on the first meeting – always try to allow yourself time to think and reflect on the interview and mull over the points and issues raised. When the time comes for the signing of contracts I would advise you to, once again, go over any policies you have and allow parents to ask any questions.

Confidentiality – It is very important that you respect confidentiality at all times. You may be caring for children whose respective parents are friends or, worse still, enemies and they may at times try to glean information from you about the other families' circumstances. You must *never* partake in gossip or divulge any information about other families of the children you care for.

Equal opportunities – You must be aware of how you can promote equal opportunities by treating all the children and their parents and families, as individuals and with equal concern. You must respect each family, their culture, beliefs, practices and religion and you must know how to discourage prejudice and stereotypical attitudes within your setting. It is important that you are confident at tackling discrimination and prejudicial remarks.

Below are examples of the policies you could use. These policies can be adapted to suit your own requirements.

BEHAVIOUR POLICY

To enable all children to enjoy their time with me I have a few requests that I would appreciate your help in achieving.

PLEASE be kind to others and polite at all times

PLEASE do not jump on the furniture

PLEASE do not run indoors

PLEASE be kind and gentle and treat others as you would like to be treated

PLEASE try to share and take turns

PLEASE take muddy shoes off at the door

PLEASE be honest and tell the truth

PLEASE REMEMBER we are all different, we have different ideas and ways of doing things and that is what makes us all special.

Fig 7.4 *Behaviour policy*

The things that you put in your own Behaviour Policy should reflect the views you have on what is or is not acceptable to *you* in *your* own home. It is a good idea to talk through the way you expect children to behave, whilst they are in your care, with the child's parents. They may have completely different ideas of what constitutes acceptable behaviour and this is something that must be cleared up early on. The children may be allowed to roam their own home in muddy shoes and eat their lunch in front of the television but, if this is something that you object to, you must make your own 'rules' clear and ask that parents help you to implement them when they are bringing and collecting their children.

The times when parents are in your home with their child are often the times when things will start to become unravelled. Children learn, from very early on, what they can and cannot get away with and which adult is the 'soft touch'. Often parents who are collecting their children after a long day at work will indulge their children out of tiredness or feelings of guilt but, if their child is using your sofa as a trampoline just because their parent is present and they know this is something you have asked them not to do, then don't be afraid of telling them to get down. *Never* allow the child to do something when their parent is present that you would not allow them to do if they weren't. It is confusing to the child and undermines your authority in your own home.

It is often difficult to know what to say to someone who is asking you questions about a child you care for. Although you do not wish to be rude neither must you breach your confidentiality policy. Politely tell the person that you are not at liberty to divulge information about the children or the families that you care for. An example of a confidentiality policy may look something like this:

CONFIDENTIALITY POLICY

You will appreciate that, as a childminder, I acquire some sensitive and private information and knowledge about the children that I care for, and their families.

As a professional practitioner I take confidentiality very seriously and you can rest assured that the information you share with me will not be passed on to anyone else (except in extreme circumstances when it may be in the interest of the child to do so).

Please help me to maintain confidentiality by refraining from asking me for any information relating to another child in my care.

Please remember that EVERYONE has the right to confidentiality and your help in maintaining this within my setting is much appreciated.

Fig 7.5 *Confidentiality policy*

An example of an equal opportunities policy may look something like this:

EQUAL OPPORTUNITIES POLICY

Regardless of their racial origins, cultural background, gender, age, family grouping or disability ALL children in my care will be:

Treated as individuals and with equal concern

Treated fairly and equally

Given the opportunity to develop and learn

Encouraged to learn about people different from themselves and to respect and enjoy those differences.

I intend to promote, at all times:

Respect of others, their culture, beliefs, practices and religion

I intend to discourage at all times:

Stereotypical attitudes

Prejudice of any nature

Negative images.

I will not tolerate, at any time:

Discrimination towards any child because of their skin colour, gender, cultural or family background, racial origins or disability.

Fig 7.6 *Equal opportunities policy*

It is important, while ensuring that parents are aware of what you will and will not tolerate from children while they are on your premises, that you also make sure your expectations are realistic and that your methods for achieving your aims and goals are effective and take into account each child's age and understanding. You must realize that no two families are alike and therefore not everyone will be in complete agreement with you.

There are many different forms of parenting and no one can reasonably say that their methods are right while others are wrong. As a childminder you must learn to understand, accept and tolerate a wide range of parenting ideas. If a parent does not agree with the boundaries and policies you have set, it is important to discuss any concerns they may have prior to signing the contract and try to compromise whenever possible.

If you feel it is necessary to revise or update your policies once you have been childminding for some time, then you must draw up a new policy, furnish the parents of the children with a copy and discuss any changes with them to ensure that everyone is aware of the changes and why you feel it is necessary to make them.

In addition to the above policies you should also set out an emergency plan showing details of the procedure you will follow in the event of an emergency and give a copy of this plan to the parents of the children in your care.

It is important that you obtain *written* parental permission for various procedures you may like to carry out within your setting. These procedures could be:

1. Taking a child on an outing.

2. Taking photographs of the children in your care.

3. Videoing an event the children are taking part in such as a concert or birthday party.

4. Transporting a child in a car.

5. Seeking medical advice when necessary.

Suitable forms seeking permission for the above can be obtained from the National Childminding Association or you could devise your own forms and get the parents to sign them.

> **Exercise:** Write a suitable policy to be used in your setting to cover the following issues:
>
> - Behaviour
>
> - Confidentiality
>
> - Equal opportunities.

Safety checks

It is important, while going about your daily childminding duties to be aware of how to continually check the toys and equipment you are using. Toys and equipment, which are in constant use by several children, will become broken and worn from time to time.

You should get into the habit of checking your toys daily; either when you get them out for the children to play with or, at the end of the day when the children have gone home and you are tidying things away. I would recommend that toys are sorted and stored in suitable boxes so that you can see at a glance which toys are kept where. This is a good way of ensuring that the correct toys are given to the correct children. For example a box which contains suitable toys for babies such as rattles, soft toys, etc., should not contain anything with small parts which could pose a threat to the child's safety. By storing your construction toys together, your puzzles and games together and your dressing-up and role-play items together you can immediately find the correct toys to suit the needs of the children you are caring for and prevent you from having to rummage through endless boxes removing unsuitable items.

In addition to checking toys you should set aside some time, say once a month, when you can spend some time carefully checking each item of equipment for wear and tear. You should make a note in your diary when the time is approaching for an equipment check and then devise a plan similar to the one in the figure below to record your findings. As well as the equipment you use indoors you should also check your pushchairs and outdoor apparatus such as swings, slides, etc. and most importantly these items of play equipment should be checked after the winter months, when they have perhaps been used very little and adverse weather conditions could have affected their safety and suitability.

Risk assessments are vital in the childminding setting and these assessments must identify which aspects of the environment and equipment need to be checked on a regular basis and childminders need to keep a record of what has been checked, when it was checked and by whom.

It is the responsibility of the childminder to ensure that all reasonable steps have been taken to ensure the safety of the children and reduce any hazards to the children on the premises both indoors and outdoors.

DATE OF CHECK	ITEM	FINDINGS	REPAIRED/ REPLACED	CHECKED BY
17 May	Construction toys	2 toys with broken parts	1 Replaced, 1 mended	Karen
19 May	Highchair	Frayed reins	Replaced reins	Karen
22 May	Potty	Split in plastic	Replaced	Karen
22 May	Outdoor climbing frame	Screw loose by ladder	Repaired	Karen

Fig 7.7   *Equipment check chart*

The EYFS statutory guidance gives three points of consideration for childcare practitioners to consider with regard to risk assessment, and these are:

- The risk assessment should cover anything with which a child may come into contact.

- The premises and equipment should be clean, and providers should be aware of the requirements of health and safety legislation (including hygiene requirements). This should include informing and keeping staff up to date.

- A health and safety policy should be in place, which includes procedures of identifying, reporting and dealing with accidents, hazards and faulty equipment.

Exercise: Make a list of the toys and equipment in your setting which will need a risk assessment carrying out on them. State how often you feel these checks will need to be carried out.

Fire drills

It is important to carry out regular fire drills while going about your childminding duties. Fire drills should be practised with the children so that they are aware of what is expected of them in the case of a fire. Children who are old enough should be taught an effective method of evacuating the house and they should realize the importance of remaining calm and doing exactly as they are told. It is a good idea to make a chart for your fire drills similar to the one in the figure below and make a note in your diary, say once a month, to practise the drill. You should change the days and times that you practise the drill frequently in order that *all* children get the chance to take part. It is pointless doing your fire drill every Monday if you have several children who only attend your setting on Thursday and Friday.

DATE	TIME	NO. OF CHILDREN	EFFECTIVENESS OF DRILL/IMPROVEMENTS NECESSARY	NEXT DRILL
Mon 10/03/08	11.15 a.m.	1 – age 3 1 – age 6months	Very effective – older child understood and carried out requests calmly.	Mon 14/04/08
Fri 14/03/08	2.30 p.m.	2 – age 2	Took a little longer than I would have liked to get the children out of the building. Decided to practice the drill again next week with these particular children.	Thur 10/04/08

Fig 7.8 *Fire Drill Chart*

Chapter Eight
Checklists

This chapter will take a look at the important procedures carried out by childminders and provide reminders of the issues which need to be addressed to ensure that you are complying with all the necessary criteria of the Early Years Foundation Stage Welfare Requirements.

Safeguarding

To ensure that this requirement is complied with, childminders need to:

- Promote the good health of children and take all necessary steps to prevent the spread of infection.

- Take necessary action when children are taken ill in the setting.

- Effectively manage children's behaviour.

- Ensure that the setting has an effective policy in place for safeguarding children.

- Ensure that Ofsted are informed immediately of any allegations of serious harm or abuse by any person living, working or looking after the children on the childminding premises.

- Ensure that suitable training is accessed with regard to child protection and that any staff employed are also adequately trained.

- Maintain a copy of the Local Safeguarding Children Board procedures and familiarize themselves with the content.

Information and complaints

To ensure that this requirement is complied with, childminders need to:

- Work in partnership with parents.

- Provide a professional service at all times.

- Ensure that they can be contacted to discuss issues when necessary.

- Ensure that the school/parents are kept informed of the child's progress by maintaining effective communication between settings.

- Ensure that confidentiality is respected at all times.

- Share written records of the children with their parents.

- Include parents in the care of their children. Encourage parents to become actively involved in their child's care and to add comments and suggestions to their child's written records.

Premises and security

To ensure that this requirement is complied with, childminders need to:

- Ensure that the premises are safe and secure both inside and outside.

- Inform Ofsted of any changes to the childminding premises which may affect the space and level of care available to the children.

- Ensure that suitable procedures are in place for dropping off and collecting children from the setting.

- Ensure that children are adequately supervised at all times.

- Ensure that adequate security procedures are in place to prevent access from unauthorized persons to the setting.

Outings

To ensure that this requirement is complied with, childminders need to:

- Ensure the safety of children while taking part in outings.

- Ensure that adult, child ratios are met while on outings.

- Ensure that written permission is obtained from the child's parents prior to taking the child on any outing.

- Ensure that a full first-aid kit and fully charged mobile telephone are taken along on any outings.

- Ensure that an adequate supply of food and water is taken along on any outings.

- Ensure that any transport methods are safe and suitable, for example if transporting children in a car make sure there is adequate insurance and ensure that each child has the appropriate seat, seat belt, etc.

Equality of opportunity

To ensure that this requirement is complied with, childminders need to:

- Ensure that they have an effective policy in place to promote equality of opportunity.

- Ensure that they fully understand the term 'equal opportunity' and that they know how to incorporate this into their setting.

- Ensure that they understand how to treat children as individuals and with equal concern.

- Ensure that they attend suitable training sessions for promoting equal opportunities and that any staff who are employed are also adequately trained in this area.

- Ensure that the setting is welcoming to everyone and that they provide positive images of male and female roles.

- Ensure that the books, toys and resources in the setting reflect the diverse society we live in.

- Ensure that they take into consideration what the children in the setting have to say and that their contributions are welcome and valued.

Medicines

To ensure that this requirement is complied with, childminders need to:

- Ensure that they have a suitable policy in place with regard to the administering of medicines and that parents have a copy of the policy.

- Ensure that all paperwork regarding the administering of medicines is accurate and up to date, and that parents sign the records and copies are maintained.

- Ensure written permission is obtained for each medicine before it is administered and that all medicines are prescribed by a doctor.

- Keep up to date with any information regarding the long-term medical conditions of all children in the setting

- Ensure that all medicines are stored appropriately and kept out of the reach of children.

Illness and injuries

To ensure that this requirement is complied with, childminders need to:

- Ensure that their first-aid training is kept up to date.

- Ensure that they inform Ofsted of any serious accidents, injuries or illnesses sustained on the childminding premises.

- Ensure that they keep accurate, up-to-date records of any accidents or first-aid treatment administered, and that parents are informed of any accidents, injuries or treatment administered to their child.

- Ensure that they have a policy in place for dealing with accidents and illnesses and that parents have a copy of the policy.

Food and drink

To ensure that this requirement is complied with, childminders need to:

- Ensure that all meals, snacks and drinks are healthy and nutritious and that balanced meals are offered to the children in the setting.

- Ensure that Ofsted is notified of any outbreaks of food poisoning which affects two or more of the children in the setting.

- Ensure that fresh drinking water is available to children at all times.

- Ensure that Ofsted are notified if any of the children in the setting are suffering from a notifiable disease or if they are believed to be suffering from one.

- Ensure that they liaise with parents with regard to their child's dietary needs.

- Ensure that they are knowledgeable about food hygiene and that they are aware of how to prepare, store and cook food appropriately.

Smoking

To ensure that this requirement is complied with, childminders need to:

- Ensure that the childminding setting is a smoke-free environment at all times while children are being cared for.

- Ensure that there is a no-smoking policy in place and that this extends to staff, visitors and parents.

Behaviour management

To ensure that this requirement is complied with, childminders need to:

- Ensure that they have a policy in place for dealing with inappropriate behaviour and that parents are furnished with a copy.

- Ensure that they never use physical punishment to chastise a child or resort to shouting, humiliation, isolation or threats of any kind.

- Ensure that any physical intervention is kept to a minimum and is only used to prevent personal injury to the child, other children or an adult or to prevent serious damage to property. Any occasion where physical intervention has been deemed necessary must be recorded and the parents of the child should be informed the same day.

- Ensure that children are adequately praised when appropriate.

- Ensure that children are allowed to learn by their mistakes without feeling humiliated or ridiculed.

- Ensure that they and any staff they employ provide a consistent approach to managing children's behaviour and that expectations are within keeping of the age and stage of development of the children in the setting.

Suitable people

To ensure that this requirement is complied with, childminders need to:

- Ensure that any person living or working on the premises are suitable to be in contact with young children.

- Ensure that their training and qualifications and the training and qualifications of any members of staff they employ are appropriate and up to date.

Safe recruitment

To ensure that this requirement is complied with, childminders need to:

- Ensure that they obtain an enhanced Criminal Records Bureau (CRB) Disclosure for all members of staff they employ or any other people over the age of 16 years of age living or working on the premises.

- Ensure that any members of staff they employ are fully checked out prior to being allowed to work with children. This includes seeking references and following them up, obtaining a full employment history, conducting an interview and checking qualifications and the identity of the individual.

Chapter Nine
Moving on

Most careers can become stale from time to time and individuals may reach the stage where they feel more challenges are necessary. Childminding is no exception. In order to stay at the top of the game and provide the best possible care for young children childminders should be continually seeking out suitable training and adding to their qualifications but what if this is not enough? What if the challenges of childminding on a daily basis no longer provide satisfaction and the job is becoming tedious? What if, when you have achieved your ultimate goal of gaining an 'outstanding' grade you no longer feel there is anything else to work towards? Is it time to get out and look for a complete change of career or is it simply time to take stock and use the experience and qualifications you have to expand your business and move ahead?

Thinking about making changes?

If you begin to question your career as a childminder it is time to take stock and decide why you are starting to feel that the career you have chosen is no longer providing you with the challenges you enjoy. It could be that you are becoming complacent. If you have received little or no feedback from parents, or if all the comments you have received have been favourable then you may be forgiven for feeling able to put your feet up and relax. This is when the job gets boring. By believing that there is no room for improvement you will lull yourself into a false sense of security and, while other childminding businesses in your area – those you are competing against – are moving forward yours will be stuck in a rut and end up getting left behind!

First, before making any big changes to your existing business you need to be sure that the service you are already providing is the best you can give. Remember an 'outstanding grade' does not mean that you cannot improve your service! This may seem obvious but, unless there is a real need to complain, many parents will be reluctant to criticize or even comment on your service for fear of offending you. However if *you* ask parents for their honest opinions you may be surprised at their response! Provide parents and children with a questionnaire asking them to make comments and suggestions about your business. (We have covered parental questionnaires in more detail in Chapter 3 of this book.) Furnishing children with a questionnaire is guaranteed to elicit some direct feedback – children tend to be much more honest and less diplomatic than adults so be prepared for some surprises along the way!

When you are completely sure that the service you are already providing is of a high standard and that the children you are caring for and their parents are satisfied with your provision, you can then begin to seriously start to think about the kinds of changes you might like to make in order to ensure that your business is moving ahead and that you are suitably challenged once more. You can then prove to the parents already using your service and Ofsted that you are a reflective practitioner intent on moving forward and improving your service all the time.

First of all, ask yourself why you feel you need to make some changes:

- Do you enjoy the job but no longer feel motivated?
- Do you feel bored and frustrated?

- Are you finding the job lonely?

- Are you finding the job too easy or too difficult?

- Do you still enjoy being with the children and providing a service to their parents and family?

It is highly likely, if you have already been inspected by Ofsted, that aspects for improvement of your business were highlighted during this last inspection. In order to gain an outstanding grade this time you will need to produce evidence that you have addressed any previously highlighted points for consideration and shown your commitment in improving your service beyond these suggestions.

Ways to expand

There are several ways you may like to bring changes into your working life without actually ceasing to childmind and these may include:

- Accessing further training

- Employing an assistant to expand your business

- Working with another childminder either to expand your business or share ideas

- Expand your own premises – perhaps extend your home or create separate childminding rooms.

You may however decide to reduce the number of hours you work as a childminder or change careers altogether, and suggestions of alternative employment may include:

- Opening a nursery business

- Working in a school

- Working for social services, the local authority, Ofsted.

When to inform Ofsted

Whatever changes you decide to implement with regard to your childminding business you will need to speak to Ofsted if you are intending to employ an assistant, work with a co-childminder or make any substantial changes to your premises or the way in which you work. Therefore your first port of call *before* making any major changes should be your local Ofsted office.

> **Exercise:** Think carefully about your own childminding business and where you would like to be professionally in one or two years' time. Consider all your options and make a suitable plan which will help you to achieve your ultimate goals.

Chapter Ten

Evaluation

Outstanding? What next?

You've done it! The feeling of smug satisfaction and utter relief washes over you as you close the door on the Ofsted inspector who has completed a thorough examination of your premises, facilities, toys, records, routines, in fact just about everything, and come to the conclusion that you are providing an 'outstanding' service! Congratulations! Pat yourself on the back for you have achieved something worthwhile. All your hard work has been recognized and paid off and you can look forward to receiving your outstanding certificate to display on your wall and your inspection report to share with parents.

But what happens next? Satisfaction you may well feel, and quite rightly so, but there is no place for complacency in this profession. Achieving an outstanding award is one thing – maintaining it is quite another and, if you wish to remain at the top of the ladder as far as providing an exceptional childcare service is concerned you will need to keep up with changes, attend training classes and *evaluate* your methods and your practice regularly. Now is not the time to sit back and let things slip secure in the knowledge that you will have no more inspections for three years. Now is the time to reflect on the inspection and think about the areas you feel impressed the inspector – the feedback you were given should help you to ascertain this – and which areas you think you could improve upon.

While everything the inspector has said to you is fresh in your mind it is a good idea to make a few notes and jot down the things you were particularly pleased with and those you feel you should act upon. If you have received an outstanding result then the inspector will feel that you are running an exceptional setting which has excellent outcomes for children, and as such the inspector will not have found any issues he/she is not happy with. However this does not mean that you cannot *improve* and *build upon* the provision you are currently providing in order to maintain your outstanding service, and it is likely that the feedback provided by the inspector will highlight these areas. *No one* is perfect and all childminders, even those with an outstanding report, should be looking at ways in which they can add to their knowledge, reflect upon their practice and develop their skills in order to go from strength to strength.

It is a good idea to share your achievement with the parents of the children you are caring for and you should furnish them with a copy of your inspection report, perhaps inviting them to comment on the content and share their own opinions with you.

By achieving an outstanding inspection report you will have demonstrated to the Ofsted inspector that your setting is highly effective in making sure that children learn through an enjoyable range of stimulating experiences in a setting which is exemplary. You will have successfully shown that you understand how children learn and develop and demonstrated a sound knowledge of supporting the children in your care in reaching achievable targets and building self-esteem and confidence.

In order to gain an outstanding grade you will need to have shown that you are well informed with regard to the needs of children and show that you have a good understanding of the importance of discussing children's progress with parents and carers and maintaining accurate written records of the child's progress and achievements.

Reflecting on practice

Unless this is your first Ofsted inspection it is likely that your previous report highlighted points in which the inspector felt, at that time, you could improve upon and, if this is the case, you will have needed to address these points in order to achieve the outstanding outcome you require. By acting on any recommendations made by the inspector you will be demonstrating a willingness and understanding of how to evaluate yourself and your practice, make any necessary changes and put those changes into effect. Typically some of the ways in which Ofsted inspectors identify ways in which providers could further improve their practice by helping the children in their care to enjoy their learning and achieve well include suggesting:

- Increasing the adult interaction with the children.

- Extending the children's imaginative play, outdoor learning and experiences for children attending the setting before and after school.

- Improving the balance between supervised and creative free play.

- Developing the use of questioning to extend children's learning – this could be achieved by asking 'open ended' questions which encourage the child to think about their answer and give in-depth answers rather than simple 'yes' or 'no' responses.

So, how can a childminder successfully evaluate their setting and build on and improve their existing knowledge?

In many cases it is often easier to improve our practice when we can clearly see where improvements are needed. However, a childminder with an outstanding Ofsted inspection report could be forgiven for believing that they need not make any changes or improvements to their practice as they are already 'perfect'. This is, of course, an inaccurate assumption and *all* childminders, whatever their grading can and indeed should be striving to improve their practice all the time. By evaluating your business and being a reflective practitioner you will be able to recognize your strengths, and identify those areas which you feel you could improve upon. All childminders will have at least one area of their practice in which they feel they could gain additional knowledge; this may be learning to be more assertive, or gaining more information with regard to safeguarding children against abuse and, in these cases, it would be beneficial for the childminder to look at enrolling on suitable training to advance their knowledge in the areas they feel are slightly lacking.

You may decide that the time is right for you to further your qualifications and a Quality Assurance programme or Foundation degree course could be suitable for you.

In order to continually improve the service you provide it is important that you reflect *often* on the work that you do rather than occasionally spare a little time to give out questionnaires to the parents of the children you are caring for perhaps because you have an inspection looming and feel this is something you *should* be doing. Reflecting on your work is something you *must* do in order to continue improving and moving forward.

Being a reflective practitioner is not simply being able to take on criticism and turn it into something positive although this is certainly a part of it. The true meaning of being a reflective practitioner is to be able to look at yourself and your practice honestly and openly, to recognize where changes are necessary and to bring these changes about successfully. To do this you need to ask yourself some important questions and answer them *honestly*:

- Which areas of my practice are the strongest?

- Which areas of my practice are the weakest?

- How do I know this? What evidence do I have to back up these assumptions?

- What complaints or suggestions have I received from parents in the past six months?

- How have I responded to these comments or suggestions?

- Was my response adequate?

- How can I access further training which I feel would be beneficial to my business?

- Do I feel prepared for all eventualities?

- Can I accommodate the wishes of all the children and their families adequately?

Of course one of the easiest ways of ensuring that you are meeting the needs of the children and their families is to ask them. Parents are usually forthcoming with suggestions and, if you ask them if they are happy with the service you are providing or if there are any areas they feel you could improve upon, they are often happy to discuss matters with you. Older children can, of course, be asked for their own opinions on the facilities and activities you provide. Try enlisting their help with planning and ask them which activities and toys they would like you to provide. It is important however, once you have sought the opinions of parents and children, that you take their comments on board and do your best to accommodate their wishes; explaining along the way anything which you feel it is not possible for you to comply with so that no one feels their suggestions have been disregarded or ignored.

List of useful websites

www.cache.org.uk

This is the website for the Council for Awards in Children's Care and Education (CACHE) and may be useful when sourcing further training and qualifications.

www.inlandrevenue.gov.uk

This site will assist with tax and national insurance queries.

www.ncma.org.uk

The National Childminding Association (NCMA) offers a wealth of help and advice to members. All childminders can purchase contracts, record forms, etc., from the NCMA.

www.ofsted.gov.uk

Office for Standards in Education (Ofsted).

www.surestart.gov.uk

SureStart is the government programme that brings together early education, childcare, health and family support. The publications section of this site relates to the government's national standards for childminding.

www.teachernet.gov.uk

The Teaching and Learning section of this site is particularly useful for childminders requiring guidance on the Early Years Foundations Stage (0–5 years) and can help with the planning of activities.

Index